TARG

LEADING
MISSIONAL COMMUNITIES
FOR STUDENTS
AND YOUTH

RICH ATKINSON

TARGET:
LEADING MISSIONAL COMMUNITIES FOR STUDENTS
AND YOUTH
© Copyright 2013 by Mike Breen

First printing 2013
4 5 6 7 8 9 10 11 12 13 Printing/Year 15 14 13 12 11 10

Cover Design: Blake Berg
Editor/Interior Design: Pete Berg
ISBN: 978-0-9846643-9-9

CONTENTS

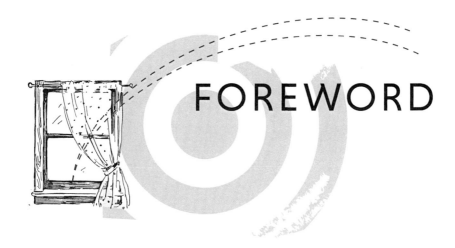

FOREWORD

"I don't know how to live without walls!"

Those are words that I don't think I will ever forget.

They came out in a conversation I was having with Junior, a Haitian man, as we drove throughout the city of Port Au Prince, Haiti, trying to find the appropriate official who could help my wife and me with some documentation for the adoption of our son Frankie. They were the kind of words that you hear not just with your ears but with your spirit.

See, in Haiti, everything is separated by walls. I encountered this unmistakable reality the first time I flew into Haiti to visit my son. After making my way through the craze and chaos of the Port Au Prince Airport, with only a minor panic attack, we jumped into the car of a missionary friend who was waiting to pick us up. We drove throughout the city until we finally found our way to the missionary compound that would be our home the next few days. But what struck me as we drove throughout the city were the walls. Everywhere we drove, it seemed like there were 14-foot walls with barbed wire around the top of them. These walls separated the outside streets from the residences on the other side of them. Inner walls separated each residence from the other residences beside it.

For most of the week, Kim and I stayed behind the walls with our son, getting to know him, playing with him and loving him. But on this particular day, Junior was helping us journey outside the walls, both to give us a tour of the city and to fill out some "must-sign" paper work. That's when we began to have our conversation.

Junior and I were talking about his recent visit to the United States, and I asked him how he enjoyed his time there. I was surprised to hear his answer. Junior said that while he enjoyed his time in the United States—eating the food, staying in the hotel, shopping at the stores, and visiting the sites—he also struggled with anxiety for most of his visit. This answer intrigued me, so I pushed him a little further. That's when Junior made this statement: "In the United States, you don't have walls. And I don't know how to live without walls." The words struck me in the core of my being and seared themselves in the center of my mind.

Living behind the walls of the missionary compound over the next few days, I began to understand more fully what Junior meant. See, while Haiti is a beautiful place, it is also deeply broken. It was broken long before the earthquake of 2010, and it remains broken to this day. Walls are what help keep people safe in the midst of the brokenness. Walls help provide a little bit of security and order in the midst of the panic and chaos that happen outside them. So, in lots of ways, it makes sense to spend most of your day and life behind these walls. To be honest, it is just safer that way.

But what Junior experienced in his trip to the United States was a different kind of society. It was one, in his estimation, that didn't have walls. It was also one that challenged his view of safety and security and left him feeling a bit anxious.

I get what Junior was talking about. I get how living without walls could be a little challenging, to say the least, because it is a completely different way of life for someone like Junior. I also know that it's not exactly true that we live without walls in the United States. We have walls. It's just that most of our walls are invisible walls of racism, sexism, classism, and the like. We have walls, and we live inside these invisible walls in order to keep ourselves safe and secure.

January 12, 2010, changed things though, for at least, a moment in Port Au Prince, Haiti. On this day, an earthquake measuring 7.0 on the Richter scale knocked all the walls down. On that day, a new reality emerged. On that day, it didn't matter whether you knew how to live without walls or not—all the walls were down. And on that day, you had to learn how to live without walls whether you wanted to or not. As a father who had a son in that rubble, I'm glad today that people did.

I tell you that story because I believe, on a spiritual level, that it is exactly why those of us who have given our lives to trying to reach the next generation have needed Rich Atkinson to write this book. Most of us who work in church, go to church, and are involved in church don't know how to live without walls. In fact, many of us have given our lives to build spiritual walls for people to keep them safe from the world outside. At best, we know how to invite people into our compounds or journey out for an occasional visit or short-term mission—so much so that we really have trouble imagining a society without them.

The truth is, there must be life without them—because, I believe we too are living in an earthquake of sorts. It's not a physical tremor but a cultural one—and it's shaking everything. The walls of truth, beauty, marriage, banking, finance, and pretty much everything we once thought could keep us safe have been shaken. People are trapped in the rubble. Even the walls of the church itself have been shaken. In fact, just 4 percent of the millennial generation is going to church. In this moment, the lives of real people depend on us learning to live without walls.

What Rich Atkinson does in this book is give us a guide to such a kind of life. More than simply inspiring us to mission beyond our walls, Rich teaches us how to live without them. And in doing so, he reminds us that what could look like our biggest threat may also be our greatest missional opportunity. In fact, as a pioneer outside these walls, Rich not only helps us see our calling to live outside them but brings the testimony of a real movement that is building on the other side.

In an age where the church behind walls is dying, the church outside the walls is beginning to thrive. As one who has spent his life calling others to journey outside of the walls and to even live life without them, I'm glad that I now have a resource to give others who have heard that call to teach them how to live this way—and even more how to thrive.

Because Rich and his team have journeyed outside the walls, his community is changing: crime is lowe; students are finding Christ; relationships are being built, and even the city itself is taking note.

I want these same things to happen in my city. And I know you do too. So, it is with great exuberance that I invite you to turn the page and begin Rich's book. I believe your entire community will be glad you did.

Dave Rhodes
3DM U.S. Team Leader

CHAPTER 1

INTRO

"Christianity is just one big stupid crutch!" Rhi said bluntly. Rhi was a 12-year-old girl who certainly knew her opinion. She shared it after I finished sharing a testimony with one of our Targets (which is our name for youth missional communities) a few years ago. I had no answer to her staunch criticism other than a childish retort: "It's honestly not!"

For this Target, we had gathered a group of young people together for an evening of fun and community in a local church building. We called this Target "Encounter" because we wanted the young people to encounter God, encounter each other, and encounter the lost. The target had about 30 young people who gathered together every week. Many of these young people had come from a single friendship circle because one Christian girl had invited them all from school. We had some fun games, which they enjoyed, and then had some community time as we sat around drinking hot chocolate, chatting about life (and providing some stuff for boys to do as we all talked). One of the leaders always shared a story of what God had been doing in his or her life over the last couple of weeks. On this occasion I shared how God had helped me through a tough time. But Rhi wasn't buying it.

Fast-forward a year from Rhi's rather blunt distrust of my story, however, and you'd see me dunking her in a swimming pool full of water with a crowd of people cheering and prophesying. God had gotten hold of another life, flipped it on its head, and brought a sworn atheist firmly into the Kingdom. Five years later, Rhi is now an amazing singer-songwriter who plays songs that bring hope and the Kingdom to young people all over our city. Even more, she recently took on the task of leading the youth work at a local church.

Honestly, I'm completely hooked on seeing God break into the lives of young people and change them by His power. I'm constantly blown away that He allows little ol' me to be involved in these young people's precious lives and faith journeys. My hope is that you'll be as hooked as I am on seeing God change young people's lives because of what He won for us.

This book is my attempt to explain the crazy journey God has taken us on at St. Thomas Church Philadelphia in Sheffield, England, over the last few years, as we have seen our youth ministry develop from reaching 60 young people a week to reaching more than 800. We have seen hundreds of young people give their lives to Jesus in one of the toughest mission fields in the country. It has been an amazing journey, as we've held onto God's coattails and learned the lessons of developing multiple communities of missional youth spread throughout a city.

Before we begin to express ideas, concepts and lessons and explore how they can transform youth ministry, however, it's important to recognize that we have learned these lessons as God has transformed our youth ministry. We have been blessed to see God breathe life into our outreach to the lost generation of Sheffield and have tried at every step to learn from our mistakes. God has blessed what we've done. We don't claim to be geniuses who have come up with some magic formula; instead, we have simply learned by watching what the Lord has done. We now feel compelled to pass on the knowledge of what we've discovered. Our hope is that you'll find within these pages inspiration, experience, and learning that will help you as you go on your own crazy journey with Jesus. We pray that you'll see transformative growth in your youth ministry whether you're a youth worker leading hundreds, a parent helping your young person reach their mates, or a pastor trying to work out how to make your church effective at reaching the younger generation.

A generation of young people is desperate for someone somewhere to share the Good News of Jesus with them in a context where they have community in which to safely process it. Seeing young people's lives changed and transformed by God is the most exciting thing in the world, and we want to help you do that based on what we've experienced. We have found that running a youth ministry based on the principles we'll explore in this book has given God room to do some amazing things in young people's lives. It's an amazing privilege to be part of the process, and I'm sure you'll find it rewarding as you read this book and share in the Kingdom stories. Our hope is that, after reading, you will see God give you some of your own stories.

We'll go through a journey together as we share the story we have been on over the last few years, drawing lessons and principles as we go and helping you consider how God is calling you to lead in the emerging generation. We'll go through the four phases of Targets and discover how the Target can connect UP, IN, and OUT at each level. Then, we'll provide a sample timeline that helps you start your own Targets. The heartbeat of this book is to provide you with all the tools you need to lead an effective youth ministry of Targets that meets young people, builds community, makes disciples, and is able to multiply. I know that this probably sounds like it's going to be incredibly complicated, but it's actually surprisingly straightforward if you follow the simple steps that we'll run through and allow God to do the hard work. Let's all begin to shoot for the Target together.

CHAPTER 2

SPOTTING THE TARGET

"Um, what do we do now?" I asked this question as three of us sat around digesting the ideas that we had discussed for the last few hours. I was sitting in our little youth office, with my key team of Dan Brown and Pippa Carter, and we were discussing the vision that we had confidently spoken out to the volunteers the previous weekend. "Seven different communities of youth work within two years?" mused Dan. We were convinced that God was calling us to have multiple expressions of youth communities spread throughout Sheffield, and we had set the target of planting six new communities within the next two years. It all seemed simple on paper, but now that we were trying to work out the plan, it seemed rather daunting.

I had been in the post as the youth team leader at St. Thomas Church Philadelphia in Sheffield for just a few months and had been seeking the Lord for the vision He was calling us to. It had been an intimidating process to arrive at a church the size of St. Thomas with a youth work charged with reaching a city—that was 66,000 teenagers! I had previously been a youth worker for five years at another church in Sheffield called the Kings Centre.

When I started at the Kings Centre, as a rather overconfident 21-year-old, I took over a youth work with a grand total of seven young people. (I can still tell you each one of their names.) I had learned lots in the five years at the local church about how to grow a local youth work with a small budget and a small volunteer base. We had seen about 50 young people come to faith in the five years, and I learned some lessons (often by making mistakes) that would stick with me for the rest of my life.

I had started out, as all good youth workers do, thinking that I was about to change the world of youth work with my stunningly cool approach. My idea was that if I built a really cool youth service, we would quickly grow a youth work that everyone thought was amazing. But after six months of trying to do a cool youth service, I learned a very good lesson: seven is not a good number of young people with which to try and put on a huge youth service. I had to set up, welcome, lead worship, preach, lead response, say goodbye to people, have pastoral conversations and then pack up. Also, worship copied from services with thousands of young people seemed a little limp with seven young people and one rather overzealous youth worker trying to hype people up as best he could.

After six months of serious effort we still had seven young people, and a couple of them had started going along to another church worship service. I needed help. Thankfully, at that point, I had one of the most powerful conversations with a young person that I'll ever have. A 15-year-old girl named Sarah and I were talking about a youth service (not ours) that she had been to the previous Sunday. The youth worker there was really cool, and they had one of the best youth services I had seen in Sheffield, with about 100 young people from all sorts of churches going. I asked Sarah how she thought we could make our youth service more like theirs. She looked at me, shocked, and said, "I don't want ours to be like theirs."

"Oh, why not?" I asked, genuinely surprised.

"Because ours is like a family—theirs is like a show," she said, looking at me like I was stupid. "I mean that's what we really want, a family."

A family? Families aren't cool, families aren't cutting-edge, and families aren't even very big. But as I started to let this revelation change the way in which I ran the youth work in our little church, we all started to hang out much more as a family. We played games together, prayed together, worshipped together, and went on family trips together. It was brilliant. I hardly had to do anything except hang out with students, and we actually grew by a couple of teenagers and got our numbers up to the dizzying heights of 11.

Still, there was frustration within me; the only growth we'd had was with a couple of friends who were already Christians. I was desperate for us to somehow start reaching some of the lost young people of Sheffield. Yet,

I was convinced about the extended family approach we'd accidentally stumbled upon, and I didn't want to start trying to do youth events again. Therefore, we came up with a plan: to start another extended family. We got some of the younger teenagers together and chatted about what fun things they liked doing. Then we put on some of the activities they really enjoyed every two weeks in the church. They invited their friends, and within six months, we had a regular 25 young people added to the older group, which continued with 11 people. Over the next five years, we added to the numbers of groups at Kings Centre using this approach of mini extended families. Over time, we had three different groups that reached about 60 young people and many gave their lives to Jesus. At that point, I got a call from Paul Maconochie, inviting me to take over the youth ministry at St. Thomas Philadelphia.

But, just two months into this new job at one of the biggest churches in the country, I found myself trying desperately to pretend to everyone around that I knew what I was doing. Truthfully, I had very little idea about how to transfer the knowledge I had gained in our small, local, neighborhood-based church to a church with the brief to call a whole city back to God. When I arrived, I discovered a youth work that was surprisingly small given the size of the church. There was one central gathering with about 35 young people attending regularly. It had a mixture of fun, worship, and teaching as well as a few other slightly disjointed bits. It was hard to tell exactly what we had.

I sat for hours with my key team members, Dan and Pippa, trying to work out what we had and how it was going. I remember telling them a few times that if only the church had an obvious neighborhood to reach, then I'd know exactly how to do it—with extended families. The problem was that the city looked so big, and the people who went to the church lived all over the place and mostly drove to get to church. This meant that there just wasn't an obvious place for us to focus on. I was struggling, and the volunteer team and senior staff were both starting to ask me what the vision for the youth ministry was. Truthfully, I didn't know. In desperation I did what I should have done a long time before. I took a retreat day and simply said to Jesus: "HELP!"

In my desperation to get away from it all, I traveled out of the city to try and hear what Jesus was saying to me. I parked myself in a coffee shop in Leeds (a city an hour's drive from Sheffield), got my pen and paper out, and waited for God to give me an idea. An hour later I had doodled, played noughts and crosses[1] with myself, and written down questions. But I felt like God had said nothing to me. Frustrated, I said to myself that if the church only had a neighborhood, then I'd know exactly what to do.

Then, as clear as day, I remember hearing God say to me, "It does. It just has lots of them." It was literally like the light bulb turned on. I made a list of all the neighborhoods of the city that had young people who were connected to the church, then I started to dream about what it would look like to see each of these neighborhoods in the same way that I had looked at the local area surrounding our church at the Kings Centre. I got excited as I started to picture extended families of youth reaching out to their local neighborhoods in all of these areas. I felt like the understanding and learning that I had gleaned in the five previous years suddenly might just make sense.

On this retreat day, I also came up with the name "Forge" to brand the youth work. I wanted something that drew on the history of Sheffield, and the city was famous for being a major steel producer in the past. Finally, it felt like I had something to present to the team of youth workers who were waiting for a vision from me.

God drew me back to my experiences at the Kings Centre. He made me realize the power of the lessons I had learned and understood that He wanted me to implement them on a potentially much bigger scale at St. Thomas'. The key piece of learning was that small, local, community-based youth work was highly effective. We had been working with a tiny budget with a small team at Kings Centre and yet still managed to see 50 young people come to faith in the five years I headed up the youth work. Our lack of budget had forced us to move away from trying to run flashy youth events because we just couldn't manage them. All we had were a few communities where young people shared life and actively chose what we did with our time. This enabled us to have real relationships, build community, and ultimately reach the lost and make disciples.

As we began to take stock of the youth work that was being run at St. Thomas', we realized that there were three key issues:

....

[1] Tic-Tac-Toe for you Americans out there.

1. We were trying to do events that were "one size fits all."

   We had a few different options of youth events that young people could go to. But while most of these events tried to serve everyone, they managed to serve no one. This led the youth ministry to constantly try to adjust the program, leaving the young people and their parents confused, burned out, and disappointed with the programs. The net result was that we were putting on several events for a fairly small pool of young people who were getting busier and busier. Meanwhile, we got more and more tired running lots of programs for hardly any young people.

   Our reflection: We needed to have multiple approaches to reach different young people.

2. Young people who came to our program were primarily from one particular neighborhood, with a few others spread from all over the city.

   St. Thomas church is located in the middle of an inner city area called Philadelphia. The majority of the teenagers from church families, however, came from a leafy middle-class suburb called Crosspool. This led to two primary issues that affected the growth of the ministry.

   First, the young people from Crosspool and the young people from Philadelphia clashed constantly due to cultural differences. We had small groups of young people from the local area coming to events at church, and because they needed such a vastly different approach, the events were typically designed to fit their needs and ended up suiting no one.

   The second issue was that the young people from Crosspool had to be driven in to the events by their parents. This made outreach to friends much more difficult. Many parents wisely carpooled, filling up the spaces in their car. If a young person wanted to invite a friend along, he or she had a logistical challenge.

   Our reflection: We needed to have different approaches for different geographical locations.

3. So many young people seemed to be living double lives.

> We were constantly frustrated with the fact that the young people seemed to be perfectly happy living lives of reverence and praise at church that didn't match their walk at school or with their non-Christian friends.

> *Our reflection: We needed the two worlds in which our young people lived to collide with each other.*

These three key reflections, coupled with my idea of running youth work based on extended family, were the basis from which we drew the most obvious idea that somehow none of us had thought of before. The church at St. Thomas' ran something called missional communities as a model. The adults were all in groups of 30 or so people in which they had community and did mission. These communities then gathered on a Sunday for worship and teaching that would aid their missional communities.

The youth work, however, still operated on a central event-based system in which we were trying to gather all the young people at the church buildings and put on the biggest events we could muster. We were a large church with reasonable resources, so we were quite good at having worship and teaching for the young people. But somehow, the youth work continued to shrink rather than grow. It had been decided that missional communities for youth wouldn't work because youth like large flashy events, so we were laboring away on these events and seeing very little fruit. Our revelation was that we needed to radically change our approach to have multiple missional communities of young people based in places where they would go without us having to put anything on.

This light-bulb moment felt like a real sense of revelation to us, and yet as we all sat around and tried to work out how to totally change the culture, all we could see were potential problems. Parents largely liked what we had at the present. They felt like their teenagers were getting lots of time with varied youth workers, getting deep teaching, and most importantly were safe in the church buildings. I knew that if I stood up the next week, shut down everything, and tried to get all the teenagers into engineered youth missional communities (which we had decided to call "Targets"), then we would have bedlam on our hands.

Question: What is a Target?

Answer: Target is simply missional community of young people. The 3DM movement that was born at St. Thomas defines a missional community this way:

"A missional community is a group of people who are united, through Christian community, around a common service and witness to a particular neighborhood or network of relationships. The group has a strong value on life together and has the expressed intention of seeing those they impact choose to start following Jesus, through this more flexible and locally incarnated expression of the church. The result will often be that the group will grow and ultimately multiply into further missional communities. Missional communities are most often networked within a larger church community. "

A missional community:

✖ can be either a new church plant or, more commonly, a subset of a larger gathered church;

✖ is centered on Jesus;

✖ has a defining focus on reaching a particular neighborhood or network of relationships;

✖ takes place in a community with lots of food and fun;

✖ has a healthy balance of UP, IN, and OUT;

✖ has a core principle that you don't need to be a professing Christian to belong;

✖ is a group unashamed about following Christ, both in values and in vision;

✖ is about being disciples of Jesus;

✖ Is a place where worship, prayer, and scripture reading are core practices;

✖ looks outward through a mixture of service and witnessing;

✖ has people gathering informally throughout the week, not just at formal meetings;

✖ has leaders who receive ongoing help, coaching, and accountability;

✖ has leaders who do not do everything but instead facilitate and release others to serve and lead.

We called our expressions of missional communities "Targets" because the phrase "missional community of young people" isn't exactly catchy. But when we talk about Targets, we're talking about missional communities—the only difference is that they're specifically aimed at young people.

We use the picture of a Target to describe these missional communities because it is a proactive concept. I used to be an archery instructor, so I taught young people to shoot arrows at a target. We would teach them to learn an initial technique that would enable them to fire a first shot at the target. Invariably, they would hit somewhere toward the edge. We called this first shot a "marker." We used this marker as the guide from which they could gradually adjust their technique until they were hitting the center. This led new archers through an intentional and necessary process of gradually changing their technique. Wild changes to the technique of the initial shot were usually counterproductive because they invariably ended up with the arrow way off target to the opposite side.

Our target to lead multipliable missional communities of young people with a clear vision of reaching young people with the Good News and making disciples. Although these Targets all look incredibly varied, they all run on the same underlying principles that we just listed. In the remainder of this book, we will explore how these principles have transformed our youth work and how you can lead your Target on the same principles. We'll talk about the four phases that every Target experiences and how to lead young people UP, IN, and OUT at each phase. And from now on, we'll refer to missional communities for young people as Targets.

As we begin, let me share a few practical details about Targets. Forge Targets typically have between from 10 to 30 young people in them. In a group of less than 10, we found that it was hard for the youth workers to build community. On the other hand, with a group of more than 30, we found that youth workers struggled to keep a coherant identity.

Many of our Targets have adult leaders who facilitate the running of the group. This is vital for younger youth, but as youth get older, we do have some Targets run exclusively by young people. We'll explore this model later in the book. For Targets with adult leaders, we have a minimum of two leaders to start with, and then, we add adults to maintain a ratio of one adult for every eight young people. This ratio exceeds suggested child protection minimums but is good for enabling a relationship-building context rather than crowd control.

Now, if you're like any other youth worker I've ever met, your next questions will be: "OK, so what do these communities do? What is the schedule? What times do they meet? Where do they meet?" You'll discover as you journey through this book that there is no one-size-fits-all answer to these questions. We have Targets that do all sorts of different things in all sorts of different places at all sorts of different times and in all sorts of different ways.

Having said that, our Targets meet at least once a week in general and usually do something that is primarily based around the Target's core outreach activity as well as something that is discipling and growing the young people in faith. The one thing we hold all our leaders accountable to is following the process of the 4 Cs by taking their community through the journey of Contact, Community, Connection, and Commission. We'll cover the 4 Cs in the next several chapters.

Now, back to the key question of how our team could go about this vision of starting seven communities spread all throughout Sheffield.

We decided that stopping the majority of what we were doing initially would be a mistake and would probably lead me to having to have a conversation with our senior pastor about how I had killed the youth work. Instead, we dropped the level of effort we put into running some of the central events and focused all of our effort into planting some new Targets. I, along with a few other people, moved into an inner-city neighborhood where we knew no teenagers at all, with the idea of starting a Target there. In fact I had a shocking moment of realizing that I had moved into a predominantly Muslim area near one of the biggest mosques in Europe.

Pippa worked with our newest staff member Rachel Whitehead, a courageous young woman of God who had once been part of my youth group at the Kings Centre. (She was one of the initial seven who managed to stick it out.) They went into one of the roughest areas of Sheffield called Shiregreen, where we knew a few teenagers through the kids' work at the church. Dan took on starting a Target called Revolution with the three 14-year-old teenagers we had left at the church at the time. These were not grandiose beginnings. We probably had about seven teenagers between these new Targets.

With the time we had gained by stripping back our current youth work, we started trying to get to know some young people. Dan gathered the three young people who had stuck with us at the church and started to go on some trips with them doing things that they said they liked. If I remember correctly, their favorite choice was the zoo—not something we would have suggested. Meanwhile, I started to prayer-walk the streets with my team and tried to hang out where the young people were hanging out. We simply started joining in their lives where they were: kicking the football around, chatting on the street corners, and joking around (usually at my expense). Pippa and Rachel did exactly the same, hanging around on the street corners with some of the hardest-to-control young people in Sheffield. We knew it was up to Jesus to make this work, or else our light-bulb idea would be shattered.

We all started with the idea of a geographical area, seeing things the same way I had viewed the neighborhood I'd been working in at the Kings Centre. I pointed out to everyone that teenagers largely stayed within a geographical area. They went to a local school, knew local friends, and played football in the nearest park. We therefore went on a hunt for where the teenagers were.

This early stage led us to our first revelation about leading Targets. (We developed the language for these revelations later as we looked back on the process that God had taken us on.) Effective Targets go on a journey, and in order for a Target be healthy from the outset, the first step of the journey is always to *make contact with new young people*. The whole point of running a Target is to effectively reach out to a load of young people who don't yet know Jesus, as well as discipling the young people you already have.

With this in mind, we all started our initial Target by looking to make contact with new local young people. Although we have more than 45 Targets today, we always start by thinking about the people we are trying to make contact with and how we are going to do it.

We'll continue to travel through the story of how God took us on a journey from these initial three Targets to having more than 45. As we do this, we will look at the example of how Jesus interacted with the disciples on the Emmaus road, and we will use this relationship as a model for how we can create effective faith journeys for young people. My hope is that the lessons we've learned will be helpful for anyone with a heart to see a generation reached and raised up to change a world desperate for another revival. Since 80 percent of revolutions are started by teenagers, I think we had better get the young people fired up for Jesus. Targets help us do this.

So let's begin to aim at the Target by digging deeper into making contact with a generation that has lost contact with the church.

CHAPTER 3

PHASE 1– CONTACT

"You're gonna get robbed!" a young person yelled from three stories up in the block of flats called the Lansdown estate in Sheffield. I had started chatting with the young lad with my team. (Well, I say chat. Actually, we yelled at each other at a volume that everyone in the block could hear because he wouldn't come down and we couldn't get up.) It turned out he wasn't threatening us at all but simply stating what he thought was obvious. It was clear to him that we weren't from "around here," and he was genuinely worried for our safety. He was actually being rather kind.

I asked him, "Where do all the young people hang out?" He replied, "At the pitch," and he pointed down the hill. Then he added, with a look of fear, "Be careful. It's where the gang hangs out." I assured him, "It's OK. I'll leave my wallet at home." Then we walked off in the direction he had suggested.

God had broken my heart over this estate in the couple of years that I had driven through it nearly every day on my way to the office from home and vice versa. I took note as every church had gradually shut its doors and moved out and as the biggest mosque in Europe had been built just down the road. I often prayed that God would send light into the area, and it turned out God answered my prayers by making me go. How often it works that way!

I moved into the area with a small team, and we had been prayer-walking and looking for young people for a few weeks before it felt like God opened up the doors for us to find some. It seemed like He wanted us to pray first because we have since discovered that making contact with young people is actually really very easy.

For years, St. Thomas' had focused on the problem of how to get young people to come to church. The answer to the question was really very simple: Don't try and get them to church—get yourself out of it. There are young people all over the place, largely with little to do. Often they are the "cause" of all the problems in local neighborhoods.

Once the young lad perched on his balcony ledge had directed us to the pitch, finding young people wasn't a problem. We didn't have to buy any equipment, organize anything, or plan anything. All we did was show up where the young people already were. This was my attempt to build one of our first Targets, and after the first ten minutes, I started to realize the scope of the task. The area wasn't the roughest in the city, but we stuck out so obviously that there was no chance of the classic youth worker pretense that we're "just like you." We therefore had to accept that we totally stuck out. We even bought matching Forge-branded hoodies to keep us warm in those cold winter months. This made us stand out even more so that teenagers could see us coming from a mile off.

As we think about making CONTACT with young people, the best thing we can do is follow Jesus' example. Let's begin by seeing how Jesus made contact with them.

> ### Luke 24:13-15
> [13]Now that same day two of them were going to a village called Emmaus, about seven miles from Jerusalem. [14]They were talking with each other about everything that had happened. [15]As they talked and discussed these things with each other, Jesus himself came up and walked along with them.

The first step on the journey of building a Target is for young people to make contact with someone who is further along the faith journey than themselves. That's what happened in this story: two men were walking and talking on the road to Emmaus when Jesus walked up alongside them and made contact with them by joining in their discussions. *"Jesus himself came up and walked along with them."*

When Jesus rose from the dead, he didn't build a temple with a big flashy banner saying, "Come and meet God here." Let's be honest: if it were up to you or me, we would probably have gone for the flashy approach of reaching the world rather than returning to the ragtag group of 11 guys who had all lost the plot when Jesus had been crucified. But Jesus went to the people who were searching and seeking.

Jesus looked to make contact with these two men as they walked on their own journey and searched for answers to their own questions. Jesus created contact with them in their own context without trying to transform their discussions, at least at first. These guys on the road to Emmaus weren't proactively seeking advice from someone to explain their exploration of life, but Jesus broke into their world and made the first move. I believe this is the pattern we should follow.

I was desperate to make our first Targets work, and it was tempting for me to think that we couldn't possibly manage to reach out to young people in the cultural context of the Landsdown estate when we were "not from around here." Then again, Jesus himself wasn't exactly *from around here* when he broke into our world and flipped it on its head forever. He was happy to make contact with anyone who needed Him, from tax collectors to lepers to Samaritans. And He did it in one clear way. Jesus didn't try and drag people into His world; He went into their worlds and got to know them.

Likewise, we realized that we didn't want to build big flashy youth clubs or worship services and try and suck the young people in. I had learned at the Kings Centre that reaching a local neighborhood wasn't done in this way. In fact, had we done this, we wouldn't actually have made contact with young people because we would have been spending all our time putting on a flashy event instead. Having young people turn up to something you're putting on isn't the same as making contact. In my experience, running flashy worship services only makes contact with young people you steal from someone else's church anyway. What's the point in that? On the Lansdown estate we had no temptation along these lines, as we didn't think we were likely to steal too many people from prayers at the mosque.

As we made contact, I was struck by the reality that young people everywhere in the world attempt to go on a journey without a guide. This leads them to draw all of the wrong conclusions about what they find and discover. Instead of having a guide, they have a barrage of false guides driving them away from the good conclusions and therefore away from Jesus. Remember, this is a battle not against flesh and blood.

Young people are all searching and seeking. They are all on a journey where they will make decisions about their understanding of the world that they will often keep for the rest of their lives. Jesus encountered two guys quite similar to the young people that we encounter. The Emmaus road guys had no one to lead them, and therefore, as they searched for the meaning held within the world, they were drawing the wrong conclusions. Jesus made contact with them and began to walk along the journey with them.

Jesus gives us a great picture for how youth work works well when done by passionate, on-fire people who can help with the searching and seeking young people go through. We have to earn the right to be heard. It might surprise you to discover that young people are not generally looking to the church for answers to their questions about life. This means that it is no good simply to put on exciting things in the church and hope that young people will come and start asking questions. We had some quite good events at St. Thomas' when I first arrived, but very few non-Christian teenagers showed up. Young people simply aren't sitting around waiting for a church to invite them to something they think is cool. There are plenty of other people putting on much cooler things than we as churches could.

I reminded my little team on the Lansdown estate every week that we were salt and light. Just by walking into the area and making contact with the young people, we were bringing the Kingdom into the area. We have to go out and make contact with young people. We have to make the first step, and the first step is listening and engaging with their conversations.

The question: How do we make contact with a generation that has largely lost contact with the church?

At this point, it is tempting to move into the world of prescriptive models of communities with methods that we have found to work. However, the very thing that we have found most effective about Targets is the fact that they can be incredibly diverse. After all, there isn't much in common between wandering the streets and going to the zoo. It would have been no good if I had told Dan that his approach of making contact wouldn't work because it was different from mine. Dan had taken his three young people on a few trips with the idea of just building some bridges with them because some of them felt let down by church. What he found was that as he asked them what they wanted to do, they naturally invited their friends along, because they were doing activities they actually wanted to do. As a result, in the context of the three young people who Dan knew, the zoo was the perfect mission tool.

But it would be daft if anybody copied the idea of taking young people to the zoo. Rather, we need to take the principle that we discovered in those early days: *young people know themselves better than we do.* When we look for methods of creating contact with young people, we always try to ask the young people themselves. As far as I'm concerned, when it comes to our volunteers or teenagers coming up with new Targets, I'm happy for our youth workers to work alongside young people wherever possible to come up with as many creative ideas as they can. Today, we have Targets in schools as lunch clubs, football groups, craft groups, computer game groups, sports teams, coffee drinking groups, music groups, and all sorts of others. The basic principle we struck upon was that it is important to get involved in the young people's lives rather than expecting them to get involved in ours.

One thing that I discovered early on in our journey is that it's important to try and keep a Target lightweight, preferably so lightweight that young people can lead lots of it. Keeping things lightweight also makes Targets far more easily multipliable. Highly complex programs that cost a fortune to emulate aren't what we're after. For a little while, we worked with some inner-city young people to run a Target where they got to do graffiti boards, DJ workshops, MC practice, girls' beauty stations, and a coffee shop all at once. Basically, we tried to do all the things the young people said they wanted to do, at all at once. This was a total failure because it took so much time and energy to set up, which meant that the youth workers had to create another youth "event" even though we were calling it a Target. Despite the fact that the church usually struggles to make contact with non-Christian young people, all of us who started our initial three Targets discovered that if you keep it lightweight and simply go where the young people are, then it's really very easy. I realize that it's not everybody's cup of tea to wander an inner-city area and get to know gangsters, but anyone can chat with a young person they know and then go and play a sport with a bunch of their friends on a local playground.

We also discovered that contact requires a different approach depending on the situation:

1. We had a group of young people whom we wanted to transition to be a Target.

2. We had a heart to reach a bunch of young people and make a Target but hadn't yet made contact with any young people at all.

Clearly, already having a group of young people that we'd like to be a Target (or multiple Targets) is a massive bonus. Young people generally have massive networks of relationships and generally have more friends and acquaintances than adults do. This is even more of a reason to put a priority on building real contact with young people beyond what happens in a program. We had run programs for the three young people who we took to the zoo, for years, and yet they had been left frustrated and disconnected from the church. These young people had been asked to bring friends to the programs for years, and yet the numbers were dwindling rather than increasing. But as we started to actually get to know about their lives and ask what things they'd like to do, we didn't even need to tell them to invite their friends. They naturally did!

We also discovered that these young people wanted to have a regular group of adults who committed to being there week in and week out no matter what was going on. As we chatted about this learning early on in our Targets, we decided to stop asking people to come and serve by signing up for a rotation. The young people didn't need different people coming to their Target every week; they needed people who would fully commit to being part of the process. As I looked back on my experience with the girl at the Kings Centre who wanted our youth work to be an extended family, I realized that the beauty of a family, when it functions well, is that the people are committed to each other.

Surprisingly enough, as we upped the commitment required for adults to come and be part of a Target, we discovered that it became easier to get people from the church to get involved. This was not something we were ready for, but as we upped the ante and asked for higher commitment, we found that adults in the church actually wanted to be committed to something. By increasing the commitment level required, we found that we got more high-quality leaders and fewer passengers who moaned and complained. I know which I'd pick any day—don't you?

Our key lesson in the contact phase of a Target was that the best way to make contact is to start really listening to young peoples' conversations and seeing if there is a way in which you can be part of the conversations and therefore part of their lives. After chatting with one group of young people, I even went to see them in their ballet (not exactly my comfort zone) in order to make this real contact. That enabled me to join in on their conversation the next time I saw them. It's not that we have to understand their world or become a part of it; I didn't rush out and buy myself a leotard. But just showing up and engaging in whatever it is that the young people are interested in is a powerful message that opens them up to the message of God, who would give up his world for one in which He didn't really belong.

Our aim became to be like Jesus on the road to Emmaus by imitating how He stepped into the conversations that the guys were having and found out what they were talking about. So many of the conversations we had as youth leaders with our young people had been based around prescriptive discussions that the leaders had set up. All those discussions got were one-word answers consisting of what the young people thought the youth leader wanted to hear. Now, our first question deals with what our young people are talking about. For example, what sport, music, TV, computer games, fashion, etc. are they discussing?

This naturally leads to coming up with a strategy, along with the young people you know, for how you can start to make contact with their non-Christian friends. We discovered that this could be anything from a standard youth club to going to the zoo. The key is that the young people drive the contact activity.

Contact strategies

"It's working," Pippa said one morning in our team meeting, as we were considering what we had seen over the last six months in planting out these three Targets. However, we now had a significant problem: we knew at some point we had to change the way our central youth event ran. This had run happily alongside the Targets we had planted, and we hadn't tried to do very much with it. It had grown a little in number and had about 40 young people turning up for a bit of worship and some fun.

We had worked hard on sharing the stories of what God had been doing in the three Targets to help the church feel ownership of what was happening. We had also shared with lots of the young people and other leaders what we had discovered. But, we knew that it was time to bite the bullet and wholeheartedly switch to a Target model of youth ministry. The most obvious suggestion was to transition our event to run as a single Target and simplify what was going on to make it more effective at making contact with new young people. But we noticed a couple of different distinct groups of young people in the youth club, which made it harder to work out what we should do. We met with parents, discussed the issue with young people, and agonized for ages. We came up with loads of ideas; all of which seemed not to work for someone.

Eventually, we came up with what now seems entirely obvious. We would split this successful club into multiple Targets. One group of young people lived in an area called Crosspool, the lovely, leafy, suburban, wealthy area of Sheffield about two miles north of the church. Crosspool offered lots for the young people to do to gain skills but few places for them to have fun with friends. The young people were busy going to sports practice, music practice, and math tutoring. These young people generally loved the youth club we had run at church and were sad to hear it might stop. So we worked with them to put on a stripped-down version of the club in their neighborhood and operate it as a Target. It was an instant hit; the young people loved the Target, and the stripped-down nature of it actually let them feel more ownership over it. They also could invite their friends because it was now down the road from where they lived. Non-Christians flooded in, and before long we had made contact with a whole load of new teenagers.

The young people who were left were from the local inner-city area and were totally different. Not surprisingly, the one-size-fits-all approach hadn't worked. With this in mind, Pippa left the Target she had begun in Shiregreen with Rachel and began meeting young people on the streets where they naturally congregated. Over time, she began another Target with some of the young people from the original group as key leaders within it. This approach began with 35 frustrated teenagers, and the Targets multiplied until they now reach more than 250 young people (we'll look at how this happened later), with scores of young people giving their lives to Jesus in the last year.

For some crazy reason, most youth workers (including myself, as you've heard already) think that we know what young people want. We tried for ages to work out what the best thing was to do for these 35 young people and then realized that there was not one obvious answer. The snag with the "youth worker decides" approach is that it seems to take a seriously large amount of effort with seriously poor results. Generally we are too quickly drawn to what looks flashy and exciting rather than what actually works— which is gathering a generation of young people who are connected with each other already and therefore tap into their contacts. By doing this, a leader can help them go, as a group, on a journey of faith. Young people aren't sitting at home on their own wishing that the church would give them a place to meet some people. So, we have learned not to try and reinvent the wheel. Instead, we simply look to get alongside the young people and listen.

Over the past four years, we've seen serious multiplication growth from our initial stumbling efforts to create three Targets. In our journey, we've explored hundreds of different ways of making contact with a generation of young people who have lost contact with the church. We found that these fall into three broad categories:

1. Detached
2. Activity
3. Schools

I thought it might be good to pause the story for a moment to take a look at these categories and share some of the light-bulb and disaster moments we have had trying to use these different contact approaches.

Detached—Starting from scratch

If we're looking to make contact with young people in a neighborhood and we don't know any, then we've found that what we call the detached approach[2] is one of the most effective, low-budget ways of making contact. It's a very simple process: we start by going where young people are and joining in on some conversations. When we started on the Lansdown estate, we simply went to the football pitch the young lad had suggested and starting hanging out with the young people that were there and joining in with what they were doing. We played football with the younger ones and

----

[2] Others, including Young Life, call this approach "contact work."

stood around chatting with the older guys who were standing around. This took a very low level of organization or effort and a small team with a budget of zero. Actually, I think I bought them a new football that cost £5 at one point, so our yearly budget was a total of £5.[3] That's not bad for a totally cross-cultural mission into one of the toughest areas we could find.

Detached youth work is where the leaders, sometimes accompanied by young people who already know Jesus and come from the local area, look for young people on the street corners, in the parks, or wherever they might be hanging out. I have seen this to be the most effective form of contact youth work amongst the urban poor because it fully immerses the leaders in the context and culture of the teenagers, enabling them to join the conversations. The youth workers walk around the streets looking for teenagers and praying for the area. When they find them, they look to join in on their conversations and to start to build relationships. This approach only works in a context where there are lots of young people hanging out on the street corners. We have found this approach to be much less effective in middle-class or rich areas simply because the young people aren't allowed to hang around on street corners at night time and get to know strangers.

If our leaders or young people are talking about reaching into a new area where the young people are primarily on the streets, then the detached approach is one of the methods I always suggest. Although this sounds like the scariest option, it's actually a lot of fun. Young people generally love people wandering the streets with the hope of Jesus burning bright in their lives.

Let me share a few key things I learned early on (mostly by making mistakes). Here are three Don'ts and three Do's:

1. *Don't try and control the environment.* We have to remember that we have walked into cultures and into environments that are not ours to control. I suggest to everyone who does the detached approach that if things start to happen with which they are not comfortable, then the best approach is to simply walk away rather than trying to stop the behavior. I've been guilty of trying to stop young people from taking drugs on the street corner only to be met with the dismissive

....

[3] That's about $8 in American currency.

remark, "What gives you the right to tell me what to do here?" The answer is of course that I have no right to tell them what to do. It also makes you seem like you have an agenda, which is a big turn-off. (As we shall see in the next section, this changes as a Target develops.)

2. *Don't try and be one of them.* One of the biggest mistakes I have made in detached youth work is to try and be as much like the young people as possible. This is, of course, stupid. I will never manage to be a 15-year-old gangster Muslim kid, no matter how hard I pretend. I was born in a pretty village in Kent. Jesus never pretended to be anything He wasn't. We have to know that it's OK for us to be different and to wander into young people's worlds so long as we're clear that we're there to listen first.

3. *Don't expect them to love you in week one.* The key to this approach is to go back, week after week, month after month. The young people often take a while to get to know us, trust us, and start to open up. For the first few months on the Lansdown estate, the majority of the young people were convinced that we were police who had been sent to spy on them. It takes a while to build enough trust to build a relationship.

4. *Do pray hard.* We always pray as a team before we go out and when we get back. I always have our youth workers constantly praying while we are out as well. This isn't just prayers for protection; we pray that God would help us be light and salt for the young people. We also pray that God would help us listen to the conversations and see opportunities that are unveiled before us.

5. *Do get involved in what's going on.* It's no good to go out and simply watch everything that's happening. Jesus didn't stand around observing people. Rather, He got involved in everything that was going on. If the young people are playing a sport, then jump in and join them; if they are chatting and standing against a wall, then go and lean on the same wall. Get plugged in!

6. *Do stay together.* We never do the detached approach as individuals. We always stay together in at least pairs, and we usually

like to keep it in trios. It's dangerous for a leader to go out alone, and even more, it's great for the young people to see us loving each other as a team and working in unison as we get to know them. If I take a big team out on a detached approach, then I still buddy people up so that if we do get split up in the evening, everyone is at least with one other person.

Activity

Most traditional youth work runs by putting on attractional activities that bring young people into contact with the leaders. This is usually done by running youth clubs with activities, games, and fun. Ours were often ineffective because they produced a one-size-fits-all model without the multiple contact points required to reach large numbers of young people.

Another issue we discovered with our traditional youth clubs as a contact point was that leaders who are disengaged with the culture of the teenagers often misinterpret what activities will attract teenagers. If the leaders ended up putting on activities that the teenagers didn't want, then the young people simply didn't come which is not really surprising. Don't misunderstand me. While I may sound negative about youth clubs, we have a number of Targets that look very much like traditional youth clubs. This is because the young people themselves wanted something that looks like a youth club and worked with us to create this space. This engagement with the process means that lots of the young people invite their friends in a way in which they normally wouldn't, even if we put on exactly the same activities.

At this early point in the life cycle of a Target, the attraction for new young people is the activity that draws the group together. As we shall explore in the next chapter, we found in our journey that allowing groups to remain in this state meant that they were unlikely to ever get anywhere. There is an inherent danger with this approach if it starts as a provider-client relationship. As we shall explore, it is vital that activity becomes less and less important as the hook for the young person. This is how you break the provider-client relationship. The more involved the young people are in creating the activities that gather the group, the less of a provider-client relationship you will have to break down later. We've discovered that remembering that our goal is to hear what the young people are talking about is the key to making this work.

Despite all these potential pitfalls, the vast majority of our Targets make contact through activity. I have seen amazing Targets that began primarily by attracting young people to come to an activity. On the surface, these appear to be traditional youth clubs, but there are several vitally important differences. You'll see them in these four key learning areas that we devised in the first couple of years of trying to run activity-based Targets.

1. *We find teenagers to drive the vision for the Target.* The best Targets are always the ones driven by teenagers. This is even the case when the drivers are young people who don't yet know Jesus but who get to know leaders, sometimes through detached work. The leaders talk with the young people to create a vision for an activity-based gathering. The reason this is vital is that the teenagers need to be the people who invite non-Christians because they have the relational depth with them to encourage them to actually come. We discovered that if the teenagers we already know like and believe in the activity that the Target is going to do, then we can be certain that they'll invite all their friends to come. We currently have a load of Targets who make contact based around activity-based Targets that do anything from football to music to crafts to youth clubs. These all have young people and what they want right at the very heart of what is happening.

2. *We stopped doing one size fits all.* Bigger is almost always not better for Target contact work. Instead, having a larger number of small, focused groups based around a specific activity is the most productive (and as we'll see later, reproductive) way of making contact with many young people. As I found in my early work at the Kings Centre, what teenagers are after is a sense of extended family. Sociologists suggest that the extended family size or social space size of people clustering is usually around 20 to 50 people. We have discovered that 50 is often too big a size with young people, so we usually suggest that our Targets are sized between 15 and 35. When they reach 30, we usually start to talk about what's going to happen next.

3. *We have learned to be prepared for mess.* As the leader of the beast that is Forge, I have found that I have to release control and allow things not to be neat and tidy. As we invite teenagers to come up with the ideas and start to drive Targets alongside leaders, we have

found that we have lots of what feel like bits of youth work rather than one flashy club. The simplicity that we once had at the center of our youth work is totally lost. Today we have multiple groups running every single day of the week in venues all around the city. Keeping tabs on it all is nearly impossible. Literally, hundreds of young disciples in our youth ministry have no idea who I am. I've never even met them! One thing is certain: the organizational headache is huge, and child protection is a constant nightmare. We have worked very hard over the last few years to make the organizational side of our scattered youth work excel. The last chapter of this book will explore this more.[4] Although this needs a little thought, if I had to choose between the simplicity of one gathering where we're not reaching the lost and what we have today, the choice is easy.

4. *We stopped making it so heavy.* The beauty of Targets is that they don't need to be the flashiest groups in the world because the activity is not going to be the basis for the group over the long term. (We'll explain this further in the next chapter on community.) We try really hard not to set up an activity that is going to be too heavy to keep running in the long term. Ideally what we want is to get young people to do a significant amount of the organization, and to facilitate this, we need to make the activity lightweight. A side benefit is that we manage to run the youth ministry on a budget that is actually workable. Whenever we talk to our secular youth work friends, they are simply gobsmacked that we can work with so many teenagers at such a minimal cost. They literally cannot fathom how we have done it. We also found out early on that the leaders that set up heavy, activity-based Targets found it very difficult to spend time listening to young people and getting involved in their conversations. If we as leaders are so busy setting up, fixing problems, and organizing everything that we can't make real contact with young people, then we're making a mistake.

....

[4] In step 8 of chapter 7, I will outline the principles and some of our practices for dealing with organization and child protection. You can see more about how we do it on our website: www. forgenetwork.co.uk.

Schools

We had another light-bulb moment a couple of years ago when a friend of mine pointed out that 99 percent of teenagers spend a significant amount of their time in school and that this fit with our approach of splitting the city into neighborhoods approach. We had spent so much time after school wandering the streets looking for young people that we'd forgotten that they all get up and go to a few gathering points of learning across the city every day. This is where their primary networks and friendships are created and based. It wasn't rocket science for us to suggest that working in and around their school was a good way to make contact with them because they are gathered in that place every day.

We've discovered two approaches when it comes to launching Targets into schools:

1. Leader-led Targets
2. Young person-led Targets

We have seen great fruit in getting leaders to work alongside young people they already know in schools to plant Targets in the schools themselves. Generally, we run these at lunchtime under the appearance of a relaxed debating society with God being the main topic. We call these "Express" and run some fun games followed by a discussion where the young people all get the chance to express themselves. We use this approach in five schools in Sheffield at the moment and have more than 75 young people gathered in Targets being discipled at lunchtime every week. As a bonus, we've discovered that the schools absolutely love us going in because it enables them to check boxes with the government about religious education.[5]

We have found, however, this approach is labor-intensive. When we first had this idea, I decided that I needed to go and start a Target in a school, so I spent a whole term calling the school every other day before we finally were given permission to go in at lunchtime. And this was in a school that had already expressed an interest in having us come!

Do to this, we have tried to run Targets where the young people run effective

....

[5] I understand that this will work differently in an American environment that is not always friendly to Christian clubs in schools. Still, I encourage you to read along and consider how you can adapt what we've learned to your local context—especially with student-led school-based Targets.

Targets in their own school without a leader even going in. This is usually most effectively done by teenagers who are at least 14 years old, but we're always looking for young people who want to give it a go. The best method we've seen is for a leader to encourage the young person to come up with a vision, gather a few of his or her Christian friends, and then come up with something he or she wants to invite their friends to do. We've found that it's always a good idea to make sure that the young people who are leading this have plenty of support and prayer from leaders who can encourage them to keep going.

Now, whenever we focus on a neighborhood, we always think through how the local school fits into the strategy —even if we're just regularly praying for the school.

Up, In, and Out

Before I continue onto the next stages of the journey that God took us on as we learned how to more effectively reach a city with the Good News, it's a good idea to look under the hood and see some basics that help underpin and balance the youth work we run.

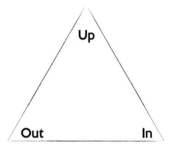

All Targets need to constantly have elements of embracing God, embracing one another and embracing the lost. We call these elements UP, IN, and OUT and use a triangle to depict them. This was learning bought to us at St. Thomas many years ago by Mike Breen.[6] As I mentioned in the introduction, I will share a little about how we've found that you need to lead at these three aspects effectively at each phase of developing Targets. At times, we were tempted to focus on just one of these elements and therefore lose the balance of the Target. But, I have found that leaving out any of these three fundamental elements at any phase makes it almost impossible to move onto the next stage of the journey. The Target stages are the ebb and the flow of the group, while the triangle is the rock over which the ebb and flow happens. This rock will have different points protruding more at different parts of the journey, but the entire rock will need to be constantly present.

....

[6] You can learn more about the triangle and how you can teach it to young people (along with other useful tools like it) in our booklet *Target — Lifeshapes for Teenagers*.

The Three CORE elements:

 UP — embracing God

 IN — embracing one another

 OUT — embracing the lost

As we explore how these three core elements function at each stage of a Target's development, I'll explain how we've experimented to ensure that we get a suitable balance to the Target without losing sight of where we are on the journey.

Up, In, and Out in the contact phase

At the contact phase of leading a Target, it is tempting to swing simply to the outward corner of the triangle and not pay sufficient attention to the other two aspects. But, it is vital that all three aspects are evident. Let's take a moment to consider how these aspects have looked for our Targets at this contact stage.

UP — embracing God

There are two key elements here:

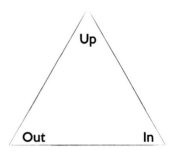

First, in the initial outreaching phase, it is vital to gather regularly as leaders, both teenagers and adults, to pray, read the scriptures, and discuss what we're seeing God do as we consider the vision of the Target that is emerging. When I led a Target reaching a bunch of young people through football, I was so focused on getting to know the young people and listening to their conversations that I forgot to pray for them with the team. We had a conversation as a team where we had to repent for not praying for them, so we decided to start praying for the young people by name every single week. As a team, we constantly remind each other that our battle is not against flesh and blood and therefore that our response to the battle should not just be a flesh-and-blood response of organizing, chatting, and working. It's more important to pray and intercede for the young people.

The second element is that we need to invest in any teenagers in our Target who already know God. We've found that the best method of discipling these teenagers is running an extra discipleship environment for them. We'll often do this before or after the Target to save on evenings, while some of our Targets meet at another time to disciple these young people. As we shall see later, setting up this rhythm is hugely effective when it comes to discipling young people who come to faith through the Target.[7]

IN — embracing one another

This is vital within the team, both for adults and young people. We've found it important to spend time having fun with each other and getting to know each other as friends. We always encourage our leaders to develop regular times when they see each other. The best way I've found to do this is to simply gather together and eat before we run the Target, pray, or strategize. Jesus was always eating with his gang, so we figured it made sense to simply copy him.

I was once running a Target, and my team just wasn't getting along very well. In the pressure of trying to love some tricky young people, we forgot that we first needed to love one another. We gathered together and aired some thoughts and then started to meet to pray for each other before we would even consider the young people. It changed the dynamic of the Target completely so that as we were making contact with these young people, they saw a bunch of people who really stood for each other and loved one another.

OUT — embracing the lost

Embracing the lost is really rather obvious in this stage. Look to make contact with young peopleand listen in to their conversations.

I have literally hundreds of stories of youth workers who have made contact with some of the most unexpected young people in the world. One of my favorites is a young lad called Zee who I met on the streets on the Lansdown estate. He was a total handful and was usually very disrespectful. We hung out and played football together on the local pitch for several weeks before I managed to have any sort of meaningful conversation with

---

[7] We'll talk more about the processing tool we use to disciple teenagers a little later on.

him. As we got to know each other, I discovered that he was seeking and searching for meaning in his life. It was amazing to see the transition from an uncontrollable young lad to having serious conversations about what was going on in his life and even praying for him for healing. It's always amazing to see Jesus breaking into the most unexpected lives.

CHAPTER 4

PHASE 2—
COMMUNITY

"Flipping heck," I said. "There are loads of them!" We'd been playing football with a few young people on the Lansdown estate for a few months, and after initially only gathering a few young people, news had spread, and more than 25 rough, tough, inner-city young people had started hanging out with us. The problem was that this group was growing and growing, which meant that rather than hanging out with the young people in their environment, we were quickly moving toward organizing a football tournament every week where we were the refs and therefore had arguments with everyone over the rules. Something needed to change. We were starting to break one of our don'ts by trying to shape the environment even though we were still running the detached approach.

As I talked with the team, we decided that the only thing to do was to look at doing something different; but we had no idea how to go about it. We knew we needed to go to the next level with some of the young people so we were not just organizing activities for them. We needed the kind of activity that would allow us to actually talk to young people instead of just being chaperones.

The next week, we all went to the football pitch, as we had for a few weeks, but we split our team into two. Half the team organized the football, while the remainder of us wandered around the edge of the pitch chatting with the young people who weren't playing at that moment. I went to a bunch of them, and they asked, "What's happening in winter?"

"Winter?" I asked.

"Yeah, when it's cold. We don't want to play football when it's freezing," the helpful young lad explained to the stupid youth worker standing before him.

"Oh, I don't know," I helpfully responded. (I thought I was a youth work genius at this point.) After an awkward silence, I asked, "What do you fellas think?"

"We could play indoors on a computer console," one of them said.

BINGO! The idea formed, and as we talked about it, I told them that if they'd help me choose what we needed to do to make it work and we led it together, then we'd start a little group of young people who could play PlayStation football together. We started hanging out every week in the warmth at a local community center and played football against each other on the console. Interestingly, they often weren't that interested in the PlayStation, and we'd end up just sitting around chatting. It was during this time that we let them name the Target and decide on what we did, and we started to go deeper in our conversations. They started to open up to the leaders, and we heard heartbreaking stories of lives without hope or future. We heard stories of struggles at home, impossible sounding choices, and childhood stories, sometimes from distant countries. All of it made us wonder how these young people were still alive. After a few months, we still played PlayStation together, but at times the guys who initially came up with the idea didn't touch the console all evening and, instead, sat around chatting over a cup of tea.

The story was the same throughout the three initial Targets we'd planted. By this stage, we had managed to hit our goal of seven communities, and this story was multiplied across them all. It was really very easy to make contact with a lot of young people using the methods that we had learned. The problem was that these gatherings were starting to feel less and less like the extended family setting we were aiming for in the beginning. We therefore all started to work on transitioning to make the activity less and less important and the sense of community more and more important.

We learned over the years that developing proactive community was vital in leading an effective Target. In one community that we called Ignition, we gathered a load of young people together based on playing dodgeball. The film named after the sport had just come out in the UK, and all the young people we knew in the area were passionate about playing. We ran a massive dodgeball tournament, and loads of young people gathered together to play.

It was a fantastic contact activity, but we realized after a few months that there was a real danger that dodgeball would become the only reason that young people came. Rather than settling for a great big youth group with little depth, we decided that we needed to make a plan to proactively move the Target to the next step by building deep community. The real problem was that so many young people had all started coming at once, and building depth and community was difficult.

We had a meeting of all the adult and youth leaders and discussed what we should do. We realized that we needed to focus on sharing our lives in order to deepen the sense of community. So, we devised a system by which we only played dodgeball for half the allotted time and then spent the rest of the time drinking coffee and chatting. We also introduced a time during this relaxed part of the evening when one of the leaders (either adult or young person) would share something that God had done in their life that week.

We knew that we had cracked the community when the dodgeball activity increasingly attracted fewer and fewer of the young people for the second half of our time because more of them chose to stay and engage in deeper conversations instead of playing the game.

This shift had to be done intentionally. We could have easily settled for having lots of young people showing up for our Target, but we chose instead to risk losing a few young people who only wanted to play dodgeball in order to build a real sense of family and community.

Leaders who can create effective community from the contacts that they have made with young people always create the most effective Targets. Initial contact with young people counts for little if the relationship does not lead to a place where a community of people can go on a journey of faith discovery together. We have had attempts at Targets that simply got stuck making contact with young people. The activity loses some young people and then simply attracts some new young people, so it feels healthy because it's not shrinking. But we realized that unless the Target moves from a phase of making contact into a phase of building deep community, then it never succeeds in making disciples of the young people whom the Target has contacted.

Once we saw this process proceed successfully in some of our Targets, we started proactively looking to create effective community amongst the young people in all our Targets as soon as a good number of contacts were made. Creating a great community gives the young people a brilliant arena within which they can process what God is saying and doing in an environment where they have real, authentic relationship. Invariably, we've found that when we failed to build successful, deep community, the enemy finds it too easy to pick off the seeds that God sows in the young people.

As I look at the young people of today, I see a desperate hunger for community. You only have to look as far as Facebook, Bebo, or gang culture to see that young people are looking to be part of something where they can express what they are thinking, feel a sense of belonging alongside a bunch of other people, and shape what their experience is. This is the environment we must create for young people if we want to see them able to grow in faith as God does things in their lives (as we shall see in the next section on connection).

After my experiences of accidentally creating community amongst the young people I was leading, I decided to take a bit of time to define what a community is to help our other youth leaders. The dictionary says a community is a *"group sharing common characteristics or interests and perceiving itself as distinct in some respect from the larger society."*[8]

I've found that Targets begin, even in detached work, as being defined by common interest: the activity, standing on the same street corner, going to the same Express Target at school, etc. But they become a real community when they share common characteristics and critically perceive themselves as distinct. The young people who are part of this community feel a sense of ownership that goes beyond just showing up for the activity offered. This is crucial because it takes the relationship between the leaders and the young people beyond the provider-client relationship to a relationship where the leader can begin to partake in conversations and challenge the status quo, therefore engaging with the young people as disciples. Since we are called by Jesus to go and make disciples, this is probably a good idea. The leader can also lead a community to other events or external programs that will help move that community to the next level, which is vital (as we'll see in the following chapter).

....

[8] From dictionary.com

We saw in Jesus' relationship with the guys on the Emmaus road how initially He simply listened to their exploration of life. At this point, He was making contact. But Jesus was not satisfied to stay in this phase. He wanted to get to the point where He could begin to be involved in their conversations, thus engaging with them as disciples. Jesus proactively sought to develop depth with the disciples on their journey.

Luke 24:25-27

[25]He said to them, "How foolish you are, and how slow of heart to believe all that the prophets have spoken! [26]Did not the Christ have to suffer these things and then enter his glory?" [27]And beginning with Moses and all the Prophets, he explained to them what was said in all the Scriptures concerning himself.

Jesus proactively gave input into the life of this little community. Remember, at this stage they did not recognize this person as Jesus. Therefore, He had to be sufficiently accepted as part of this new little community so these travelers would receive His input and explanations. Now, let's see how these guys accepted Jesus as a part of, and even as a leader for, their new little community.

Luke 24:28-29

[28]As they approached the village to which they were going, Jesus acted as if he were going farther. [29]But they urged him strongly, "Stay with us, for it is nearly evening; the day is almost over." So he went in to stay with them.

Jesus gave the guys a choice. He had developed the relationship to the point where they were pushing back to Him and asking for more. Jesus didn't force Himself upon them with an ever more impressive event or list of explanations. He allowed them to accept Him as the leader and to accept the entity as a community. In my observation, most youth workers can happily create a contact point with young people, but to build effective community needs a little shove in the right direction.

I've found that the best way to measure community is to consider how committed the young people are to the group because of the activity and how committed they are because of the relationships that they have in that environment. A Target can still have a strong activity basis or focus, but we know that it is moving forward to being a full-fledged community the activity stops being the hook for the young people and the community becomes the thing that keeps them engaged.

A really helpful barometer of the strength of the community aspect of a Target is to consider what would happen if you changed the activities that you ran. Would all the young people come despite being frustrated with the activities, or would they simply go and find somewhere else to fulfill their desire for fun? Would they discuss how they might change it together with their leaders, or would they never be seen again until we built something really cool? This can be a hard thing to measure, but we have found that it's always worth consideration.

This is important because we need to be able to challenge and push the young people in our Target to be youth workers who are successful makers of disciples. If they haven't decided to be part of the community, then they will leave at the point of challenge and initial shaping by those who know God.

The good news is that young people are longing for community. It doesn't take a large amount of research to see that young people are hungry for community but often find it in the wrong places. They tend to find communities that drive them away from the one answer that will actually help them. They are looking for places where they are loved, accepted, led, part of something, and free to explore the world. You only have to look at the rise and prevalence of gangs in urban centers to see how this works. Interestingly, these gangs usually run through a similar process to the one we're describing here. Gangs usually gather young people by making contact with them on the streets or by hanging out and playing sports or running low-level crime. These groups then become communities that are not simply defined by activity but by identity, acceptance, exploration, leadership, and common purpose. Every young person is looking for community, and therefore it's not difficult to create it.

I've taken a considerable time to examine what it is that helps us create effective community among the young people with whom we have made contact. My reflection is that there are three things, when done well, that indicate we've created effective community. They are:
1. Commonality
2. Distinctiveness
3. Relationship

Commonality

The first question we have to ask ourselves is what we have in common. This can be anything from an activity, an area, a type of music, a program, a belief, a debate, a meal, etc. It really can be anything. Usually, youth groups and youth leaders struggle to create a community because they do not allow commonality. Most youth programs try and do so much in one evening that it's almost impossible for there to be one thing that all the young people can sign up for and say, "Yes, that's us!"

I've also found that it's best not to be overly spiritual about this or come up with scripture attached to our church's vision statement. I try to remember that in order for non-Christians to feel like they can be part of this community, the commonality needs to be something that everyone can sign up for. Of course, avoiding over-spiritualization doesn't mean that the community isn't based around Jesus. Jesus is at the center of everything that we do. But in order for non-Christians to feel like they can be part of the community, they need to share in the commonality. Our leaders began to name and shape all their Targets around the idea of the shared commonality. This was a simple strategy and made it so that anyone could sign on. That in turn made growth easy and future multiplication possible.

Our commonality on the Lansdown estate was that we played football on the PlayStation. If you asked any of the young people in the group what we were about, they would have answered that we were about playing computer games. As mentioned previosuly, I also ran a Target that looked like a very traditional youth club, but the commonality was playing dodgeball. Ask any of the young people who were part of that Target what we did as a community, and the first thing any of them would say is that we played dodgeball.

Distinctiveness

What makes a Target distinctive? As we've seen, community only becomes fully formed when it sees itself and is seen as *"distinct in some respect from the larger society."*[9] To put it simply, it has an identity. Our Target leaders spend time trying to work out what is distinctive about the Target so it can

....

[9] From dictionary.com

be belonged to. This usually includes coming up with a name, a logo, a badge, or a brand. We have found that it's counterproductive to do this as a complicated process with art designers and 500-run T-shirt printing. Instead, we sit with the young people and come up with a name together, and then maybe get someone to design a logo or a flyer. You'd be amazed at the power of having a shared name. If you're wondering how important this is, take a look at every major inner-city gang. Every one of them will have a name, a tag (a kind of logo that they graffiti), and often a social-media page that explains their distinctiveness and commonality.

We almost always try and go through a shared process of naming, branding, and forming the community. We do this instead of coming up with something and then presenting it to the young people. So we sit together and come up with the name and brand alongside the young people because this kind of collaboration is a better way of building community. All of our Target groups have a name and usually a logo, and most of them are chosen by young people.

We have also found it really effective to give the young people a wider brand within which they can brand their Targets. Our flagship brand is called Forge Youth. All of our Targets hang off the Forge Youth brand and give the young people a wider identity within which they can personalize their own group without losing the connectivity of being part of something bigger and wider. The wider brand just gets stamped in a small logo on everything else that is produced and keeps everyone feeling part of something bigger and wider. We spent a lot of time thinking about branding, and I'd advise any youth worker to think carefully about how they can create brands within which there is flexibility to personalize the brand at a local level. Multinational companies have great success with a similar process, so it makes sense for us to learn from what they have gleaned by spending millions on research.

Here's one example: In their advertising of Windows 7, Microsoft tried to tap into the way in which today's culture longs to feel ownership and personalization of the meta-story of a larger brand by using the phrase, "I'm a PC, and Windows 7 was my idea." The commercials focus not on the overall features of Windows 7 as in previous generations of ads but instead narrow in on specific small ideas that individual local communities have suggested. This is an attempt to connect a global product with local individuals and communities. Microsoft is trying to show how it listens to the local people, and therefore the global brand becomes a powerful place for individual and local communities to operate.

We've discovered that creating this kind of meta-brand within which Targets can operate creates the strongest and safest environment to operate youth work. This has also accidentally had the effect of giving us a much larger presence in impacting our city. Lots of, what could have been, disconnected pieces of missional youth work would have little impact on the city as a whole. But a connected network of these Targets under a brand means that the authorities and power holders of the city sit up and take notice. Forge Youth is now well known by the chief superintendent of the police, local government officials, and most churches in the city. This connected and yet disparate approach has enabled us to hit a sweet spot of real, vibrant, community-centered mission combined with the advantage of being a larger organization.

Relationship

I asked one of our Target leaders, "What level of relationship does everyone have?" The leader was scratching his head and trying to work out why his Target was struggling to move forward. He replied, a little dejected, "Shallow at best." "In that case," I responded, "Make sure you make your program less exciting."

I've had this conversation what seems like a hundred times in my nine years of youth work. Sometimes I've had this conversation with the Lord, as I've tried to remember what I should be spending my time doing. Most youth workers I speak to instinctively know that building good, strong relationships is the key to effective youth work. But youth work easily becomes all about running effective programs, and the result is that youth workers (both paid and voluntary) end up so burned out that building deep relationships with the young people and enabling them to have healthy deep relationships with each other gets completely forgotten. We try and remind each other as a team all the time that the only way to build real community is to build deep and real relationships. This works both between the youth workers and the young people and among the young people themselves.

In order to effectively share a sense of commonality and distinctiveness, we've realized that we need to have a depth of relationship with others in the Target. This isn't just between the leader and individual young people but between everyone in the Target. Our leaders spend almost all their time looking for opportunities to foster deeper relationships. This is usually done best by offering the chance for extra time together—basically giving them the chance to buy in more.

When I was building some of my Targets, I would literally sit in a coffee shop after school, and young people would drop in and hang out and talk about how their day had been going. A trip, excursion, extra discussion times, and time to eat together before an activity are all effective ways of developing this extra time and buy-in.

The other way to develop deeper relationships is for us as leaders to start to share more the deeper parts of our lives. I've often shocked young people by sharing with them times when I've struggled or when things have been hard. While this may surprize some people who suggest that as youth workers we should pretend to have it all together all the time, it seems unfair to me to ask young people to make the first move. Jesus didn't exactly sit in heaven waiting for people to sort themselves out. He came and shared his life with us, a life that "first loved us." We can't expect young people to share their lives with us if we're not prepared to share something of ourselves with them.

This creates an environment and gives permission for others in the community to open up as well. Teenagers seem to come equipped with truth radar, and the one thing they seek more than anything else is authenticity. We often talk as a team about the importance of not pretending in front of the young people but instead simply laying our lives out before them, including our worries and fears. Usually I find that young people respond better to youth workers who operate with vulnerability and who offer themselves with no front or pretense of being cool than they do to youth workers who try and pretend to be really cool and have it all together. This generation has seen the mess caused by their parents' generation up close and is under no illusion that life, people, and adults are perfect. If you pretend to be perfect, they'll back off and presume that there's something wrong that they can't see. But when they see your fear and weakness unveiled, they'll trust you with their fear and weakness.

The only caveat I would raise at this point is that it's important for youth leaders not to use young people as counselors for the mess in their lives. It's fine to tell them what's going on, but the Target is not an environment to get help and guidance when we need it. Over the years, I have had to suggest that a few people go and get pastoral advice and help from the church before they continue in youth work because the Target was becoming defined by their issues. It's important for us to be open and vulnerable without looking for answers from teenagers or using the Target as a place to dump our problems. I always make sure that before I share something with young people, I've talked it through with older and wiser heads so that I can make sure that what I share is appropriate.

Discipline

Discipline in youth work is a massive issue, and it might seem strange to place it here in the flow of this book. But, I have realized that the process of building effective community through commonality, distinctiveness, and relationship is the key to effective discipline within the Targets we run throughout Sheffield, regardless of what type of Target they are.

I learned my best ever lesson in discipline from Ruth: Ruth was coming to one of our Targets, and she was a real handful. She had been expelled from a couple of schools and knew how to cause trouble. We had lots of little chats where I had to pull her to the side and discuss her behavior. At the end of one of our evenings hanging out as a community, she was walking past me to leave, and I said "It's been really great having you here tonight, Ruth." She turned and looked me in the eye and said dismissively, "Yeah, right." I looked her directly in the eye and said, "From the bottom of my heart, I love having you in this group." For a moment, we stood staring at each other. To this day I'm convinced she was waiting for me to turn it into a joke. Once it was clear that I wasn't going to, she turned and ran off. She came back week after week after that, and we hardly had any trouble from her again.

I constantly get asked about how to do discipline in youth work. I can say that in nine years of youth work, the only really hard discipline issues I've faced have happened when we've failed to build effective relationship and community. If we get these two elements right, it's almost always surprisingly easy to maintain discipline even amongst some of the toughest teenagers in the world.

I have found over the years that young people who cause lots of trouble are often simply seeking attention. They have often learned that the only way of gaining attention in their lives is by causing trouble. I remember a young lad called Jimmy who started to attend one of our Targets several years ago and was renowned for being quite a handful. Initially, we found him to be tough work too, but we found that as we gently set the boundaries, accepted him into the community, and worked hard on giving him more attention when he was engaging well in the community rather than only giving him attention when he was causing trouble to the Target, this behavior began to change.

If Jimmy had attended a standard youth club where the heart of what was going on was the activity itself, then we would have constantly battled with him to make him behave. It was amazing to see this young man who had struggled and left school because he couldn't engage with the rules and structure relate well in the context of a well-built Target community. To cap it all off, it was a joy a couple of years after him joining our Target to baptize Jimmy and even more of a joy to see him still going on with Jesus to this day.

A key lesson I've learned is that if we build community in the way I've outlined above, we find that the young people will do a lot of internal discipline without leaders even having to get involved. If they feel a sense of belonging in the community and find identity in it, then the young people themselves will naturally want to self-police. They won't want to let things get out of hand because it will ruin it for them and for us. Remember, we're all part of the same community. We're the designated leaders, but that simply means we'll sort it out only if we must. Obviously, this doesn't mean we never have to get involved in situations, but it does make it much easier. If the young people own it in the Target, then they'll own it when it comes to discipline.

The second tip we have is to build deep relationships. The deeper our relationships with young people, the less trouble they will cause us. If we have relationship with a young person, then simply asking him or her to stop what they're doing is usually enough. I find that I hardly ever have to raise my voice with a discipline issue. In fact, I generally find that the people who try and shout at young people actually lose control.

By far, the biggest mistake I have made myself is one that I constantly see others make—going for an environment where the leaders cease to be able to effectively develop relationships and community and therefore simply become police. When that happens, the Target descends into an us-versus-them stand-off between the young people and the team. If this develops, we never effectively make disciples and will constantly have discipline issues. Young people know what to do in the us-versus-them environments created for them at home and at school, where people with way more training and experience than most youth workers struggle to keep control. But by creating simply an "us" environment, we've found we have far fewer issues.

I remember one time in one of the roughest Targets I ran, a computer console game pad was stolen by one of the young people. I had no idea who had stolen it, and I was frustrated with whoever had done it. I talked with the young people as a whole and explained that we didn't have enough money to buy a new one, so we as a community would have to go without for a while. The young people were furious, not with me but with whoever stole the pad. They couldn't believe that anyone would steal from our community and were desperate to find out who had done it. Whoever it was managed to hide away amongst the community, and we never saw the pad again, but we hardly had any other issues after that. I think that whoever had done the thieving was so terrified by the strength of feeling by the young people in the community that he or she wouldn't dare try it again. These were young people who had no problem with the concept of stealing (many were in local gangs that regularly stole), but they had a strong sense of loyalty to the community and therefore couldn't understand doing it to themselves.

There are obviously times when young people step over the line, and we need to step in and stop them. I have sometimes had to make sanctions, such as banning them from the Target for a week or more. The key thing I've found is that if I make threats of sanctions, then I always have to follow through with them if the young people cross the line again. The trick with this is to try and have a one-on-one discussion with the young person. Whenever I've made a fool of them in front of the whole community, then I've always gotten a terrible response. If I do get to the point where I need to expel them for one reason or another, then I always make sure I make it clear that I'm gutted that I had to do it for the good of the community.

We've found that as our teams develop great relationships with young people and build effective community, our issues with discipline have been greatly reduced.

Up, In, and Out in the community phase

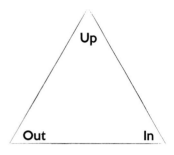

As previously mentioned, we have discovered through much trial and error that it is vital to include aspects of UP, IN, and OUT at all times for a Target to be effective. Now let's consider how to do this in the community phase.

UP — embracing God

As we build community in our Targets, we have found that it's important to continue with the ways of embracing God outlined in the contact chapter. In addition, it's important for the leaders and Christian young people in our Targets to begin proactively sharing our stories. Building deeper relationships comes from being vulnerable and sharing what God is doing in our lives, and testimony is a great way of doing this. We've done this either by having a structured time when we share what God has done in our lives or by getting all of our leaders to be intentional about sharing their stories in their chats with the young people during the activities.

I've been asked hundreds of times for advice on how to do this in a way that isn't overbearing but that works for young people. I have found that the most effective way to do this is to obey three simple steps I call "Keeps":

Keep it short — It's no good to go waffling on for ages. Get to the point and tell them what God has done.

Keep it personal — It's totally pointless to share everyone else's stories. These can seem more exciting than our own, but I can promise you that they are far less powerful than us sharing what God has done in, through, and with us. Remember that we're opening community by being vulnerable with our lives. It's also easy for young people to dismiss a secondhand story. When a story comes from someone they have gotten to know, it leads them to decide whether we are mad, bad, or telling the truth.[10]

....

[10] Some Americans may need a different way of saying "mad, bad, or telling the truth," which is an important phrase in our Targets that will show up again later in this guide. Think of C.S. Lewis' writings on whether Jesus was a liar, a lunatic, or Lord, and you get the idea.

When we get to the next stage of connection, we'll often use this mad, bad, or telling the truth challenge with the young people who have heard stories from their leaders and Christian young people.

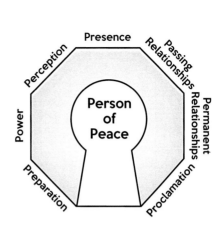

Keep it recent — I've found that it's far less powerful to tell young people what God did in me 10 years ago. Whenever possible, simply share what God has done in the last few weeks. This is also a fantastic challenge for us as leaders and team members because it forces us to keep our eyes open for what God is doing. God is constantly working in us and speaking to us, so we should always have something to share. It's all part of the Good News that the God of the whole universe is constantly at work in our lives.

We have learned that by sharing these testimonies, we are really upping the spiritual warfare for young people. Revelation 12:11 says, *"They triumphed over him by the blood of the Lamb and by the word of their testimony; they did not love their lives so much as to shrink from death."* Sharing testimonies is massively effective, but there is always a battle that happens in our minds when it comes to actually letting it out. The challenge we must face is not to love our lives so much as to shrink from being slightly embarrassed.

I once spent a whole year in one of my Targets doing a section during the evening called the Hot Spot in which a leader or a Christian young person would share what God had done in the last couple of weeks. This time was never more than two minutes long, and it never seemed like the young people were listening. But after a year, we ran a discussion group alongside the Target for young people interested in discussing faith, and to my amazement more than 25 young people came to the discussion. When I talked about giving their lives to Jesus, three girls told me that they already had done so just from listening to the testimonies. There was a party in heaven, and we hadn't even noticed!

IN — embracing one another

The community phase is where the in activity goes into hyperdrive. We look for anything that will build commonality, distinctiveness, and relationships, as we've described. At this point we often notice that certain young people seem to be particularly drawn to us and want more time and depth than others. We've found that when this is the case, then they are probably our key "people of peace."[11]

Matthew 10:11-13
[11]Whatever town or village you enter, search for some worthy person there and stay at his house until you leave. [12]As you enter the home, give it your greeting. [13]If the home is deserving, let your peace rest on it; if it is not, let your peace return to you.

As we notice these key young people, we always get our leaders to make extra time for them. We make the effort to arrange to meet them separately for coffee, McDonald's, or in some other public meeting place. This is an excellent way of developing deep relationships with young people who are often the key holders to many other young people and who can often help you lead the rest of the group.

I was once really struggling with the community within one of our Targets. We had tried many things, and yet we still felt like a disparate group of young people without real focus. One of the key and most influential young lads named Jimmy randomly asked me if I could go for coffee with him and help him write his CV.[12] We spent a few weeks meeting up and working on his CV so that he could try and get a job. He loved it, and we started to develop a really good friendship. The very fact that he was so influential in the Target then made life much easier on us in terms of developing community. He was on my side, and all the young people simply followed his lead. As we then moved to trying to name the Target, suddenly all the young people were really up for the idea. From then on, I have always looked for the person in the group who might be the person of peace.

I was once running a Target where we as a leadership team became so close that we were meeting together a couple of times a week to eat together and pray together. Although this level of activity isn't my usual experience, it's really important that we as leaders stay close. You'll need to make sure you spend a significant amount of time with your team praying

....

[11] For more on the Person of Peace tool, read *Target — Lifeshapes for Teenagers*.

and eating together so that you are operating in community as a team.

OUT — embracing the lost

At this point in the development of a Target, we have obviously already made a lot of contact with young people who don't yet know Jesus. The Target is obviously not closed to new people, and often the young people who don't know Jesus are the best people in the world at getting new young people to come and make contact. I've found that it's worth helping them do this by giving them aids to do so. We always arm our young people with flyers (which often they'll create) that they can hand out when inviting their friends to come and be part of their community. This helps the young people who get invited remember what they've been invited to and reminds the young people to invite them. It's usually a natural process for teenagers to do this because they have strong relational networks, often based through their school, and because they are used to inviting others to activities in which they are involved. The key is simply to enable them to do this natural process as well as possible.

I was running a Target that had already grown significantly to about 15 young people, and we were working hard on creating a strong sense of community. As we developed the community, one girl gradually invited her entire friendship group. This grew the Target to more than 30, and we were baptizing most of her friends a couple of years later. It's amazing what God does even when we're not looking for it.

We've found that it's easy to be so busy with all the practical aspects of running a Target that we forget to be praying deeply for the teenagers. I always get my teams to pray earnestly for the young people they have in their Target. We often write down their names and start praying for them by name every week, sometimes distributing the names amongst the team and getting them to commit to praying for a specific young person for as long as they commit to the Target. I think that it's really exciting to do this because the young people sometimes have never been mentioned by any saint before the Father before. We might be the first. It's time to battle for these young people.

....

[12] Curriculum vitae, also known as a resume.

CHAPTER 5

PHASE 3–
CONNECTION

"Your youth work is massive," a friend of mine said as we were
out for a coffee. I was explaining what God had been doing in Targets
expanding all across Sheffield. We had already gone from just a couple of
Targets to more than 20 meeting regularly, and we were pulling in the lost
from all over the place. These had mostly become wonderful vibrant, real
communities as the leaders had taken what we had learned in our early
Targets and made great contact and then developed that contact into deep
community. We were growing like crazy, which felt really exciting, but I had
a nagging thought in the back of my mind: Were all these young people
hearing the Good News of Jesus? We were gathering hundreds of young
people in these communities of around 30, and they were hearing stories
of faith from the youth workers, but I was worried by the fact that very few
seemed to be giving their lives to Jesus. We had staked an awful lot on the
multiple-community model, so I was terrified that we might see very few
young people actually giving their lives to Jesus. "What's the point of just
having a big youth work?" I wondered.

I looked at all of our Targets and talked to lots of our leaders to try and find
out what was going on and what we could learn from the situation. The
answer was obvious: We needed to be more intentional with the challenge
of the gospel. Once our young people had heard the testimony of Christians,
they needed to get to the challenge of whether they thought these Christians
were mad, bad, or telling the truth. If they thought the Christians were
telling the truth, then they also needed the challenge about how they would
do something about it. We were seeing some level of breakthrough, but
it was only happening in certain groups. As I looked at these groups, I
realized that these groups were always run by people who had naturally

challenging personalities and who therefore brought the challenge of the gospel. I discovered that these people often struggled with the earlier stages of contact and community because they were always so keen to get the challenge of the gospel out to the young people. This sometimes meant that they scared the young people off with a big-hitting challenge before they had really listened to their conversations and built deep community.

I told my colleague Dan, "There must be a sweet spot," as we mused about the problem. "Young people often give their lives to Jesus at an event," Dan offered as we discussed places where we had seen lots of young people making commitments. That was it! Light bulbs came on, and we came up with the vision of running a big event where all of our Target leaders could gather all of their young people to have a night of fun and hear a really good gospel message. We decided that this couldn't be regular, because it would take momentum out of the Targets, but we could do something every once in a while that would help move all of the Targets along to the next level of helping the young people make **a connection** with Jesus. Thus, the vision for Glory Revolution was born. It was a night of music, and I preached my heart out, with loads of young people giving their lives to Jesus at the end. We then sent them back for follow-up within in their Target communities. To be honest, we messed up nearly everything on this first gathered connection event, but so much groundwork had been done with young people in the Targets that many were totally ready to give their lives to Jesus. God was very faithful to us.

This experience helped us realize that beyond just making contact with young people and building deep community, we absolutely had to seek to help them get connection with God. Since our initial purpose was never to have a massive youth work but rather to see young people's lives changed by God, this should have been totally obvious to us. It certainly was obvious to Jesus in his connection with the men on the road to Emmaus.

> *Luke 24:30-31*
> [30]*When he was at the table with them, he took bread, gave thanks, broke it and began to give it to them.* [31]*Then their eyes were opened and they recognized him, and he disappeared from their sight.*

Let's remind ourselves of our Target. We want to see young people connect to their Savior. So quite obviously, this connection is the next stage of the journey for our Target. We know that the best thing that will ever happen for young people is to meet with God and get to know him as their Heavenly Father, their reason for living, and their hope for the future. I hope that you agree with me that this is our heart.

So the question is: *Why on earth have so many young people never heard the Good News, even when they've been in youth groups for years?*

This situation is perplexing to me. I see youth workers who are good at making contact with young people and who have built successful community from those young people but who never seem to be able to make the leap to see young people give their lives to Jesus. The trap that I see youth workers fall into is twofold:

They fear that young people will leave.

Often youth workers who run communities don't challenge young people with the gospel because they fear that some will leave. But the truth is, unless God does something crazy, some will almost always leave when the community is confronted with the gospel. Salvation is God's responsibility and not ours, and therefore the fear of losing some young people should never be an issue. Merely meeting young people and having them in community is not our goal. Why would we stop when we haven't met our goal of making disciples?

I think it's fine if young people leave a Target because the spiritual temperature is raised. There have been loads of young people who have left my Targets over the years. This is always a gutting process, but as leaders, we have to hold the big picture of what's going on in front of us and know that we are using the marker of community to shoot closer to the bull's-eye of connection. So even if our youth community shrinks a little, it's actually closer to the target than before. One of the most common conversations I have with our Target leaders is telling them to raise the temperature and challenge and expect a shrink in numbers.

I was chatting with one of our young people who had been part of one of our Targets when a whole load of her friends became Christians. She was a signed-up atheist and was livid that we had hoodwinked her friends. She left the Target and decided to never return. However, you might be able to guess that since I was having a conversation with her, she eventually did return. She came back six months later because she simply couldn't get past what she'd seen God do in the lives of her friends and how they had changed for the better. She's now going for it as much as any young person I've ever met, and she's passionate about seeing young people find the hope she has found in Jesus. If we had spent all our efforts trying to dumb down the Target to work for her at the moment when her friends had come to faith, then we probably would have lost her anyway, and we wouldn't have discipled her friends properly. By focusing on discipling the people of peace, we had accidentally created another one, even as she watched suspiciously from afar.

They don't know how to bring the challenge

It can be really difficult to know how to bring the challenge of the Good News in the context of a Target. This can be hard for the person who has built up the relational trust and worked hard to create the community. And different leaders have different gifts, which means that some find this process more difficult than others.

What is the Good News?

Let's take a minute to examine the message of the Good News. For years, when I tried to share the Good News, I made it incredibly complicated. I told young people that they were sinners and tried to explain the trinity and the cross and hell and heaven and as much theology as I could squeeze in. This was usually met with a confused response along the lines of, "And why does that affect me?"

The truth is that the message of the cross fails to affect young people not because it is not powerful but because usually they are starting from the point of view that there is no God at all. Therefore, they don't understand sinfulness, hell, heaven, the trinity, or why on earth these ideas have any importance to them.

Jesus made the gospel simple, and so should we. The Good News doesn't have to include lots of theology to explain how it all works. Young people simply need the bare bones. Here's how Jesus put it in Mark 1:15: *"The time has come," he said. "The kingdom of God is near. Repent and believe the good news!"*

If Jesus' message was so simple, then I find it strange that we manage to make it so complicated. I'm not saying that young people don't need to understand the whole process of Jesus' death and resurrection at some point. It's just that they don't need it at the very beginning. All Jesus seemed to tell people was that they could meet with Him (the Kingdom of God was near) and that they should turn around (repent) and go in a different direction (believe). This is the Good News of the cross made very simple. We have to trust that the message of Jesus is simple, powerful, and effective and that if we deliver the same challenge, then God will challenge hearts without the need for complicated doctrines.

We always work toward this simple message and then ensure that good discipleship is in place through the community so the fundamentals get worked through after young people have had the initial experience of meeting with God as they turn toward Him and begin in faith.

Event and Process

My observation is that, however slow the journey, every believer has an event or moment in his or her life when he or she decides to accept Jesus into his or her life. Look at the guys on the Emmaus road: there was a moment when "their eyes were opened and they recognized Him." I have seen time and time again these moments when young people's eyes opened and they recognized Him.

There is no one way of introducing challenge to a Target, but I want to talk about two specific ways I have seen Targets do this successfully:

The first is through a Good News event. After our experience with Glory Revolution, we now run a number of events that allow our Target leaders to bring their young people to an event where leaders know the young people will have fun and hear a clear gospel message with the chance for a response to the challenge. The leaders use their relationship with the young people to suggest that they go as a community to one of these centrally run events that best suits their young people. They go as a Target community and process together afterward as well. This takes away the hit-and-run aspect of big events and actually fosters a great discipleship environment.

All of our Target leaders are encouraged to look for an event where the young people will have fun and hear the Good News in a simple way that will challenge them to consider whether their leaders are mad, bad, or telling the truth.

The second way we have found to challenge a Target with the Good News is for leaders to do it themselves in the Target. This can be done in a couple of ways. The first is to gradually take the entire group on an exploration together. Usually this starts by introducing testimony and ends by explaining that God is here and offering young people the chance to respond. It's key to make the response really clear and to ensure that you actually get to the point of asking if anyone wants to give his or her life to Jesus. I have been amazed, whenever we share the Good News, how young people always give their lives to Jesus.

We have tried to help our leaders by putting a resource together called Truth Revolution, which is a six-part DVD set that takes young people in some of our Targets on this journey from no faith at all to making a commitment to changing the world with Jesus.

One of the phrases we use all the time to help our Targets stay on track in the connection phase is this: *The Good News is called Good News because it actually is good news.*

Let's see what this event and process looked like for Jesus with the men on the road to Emmaus.

> ### Luke 24:32-35
> [32]*They asked each other, "Were not our hearts burning within us while he talked with us on the road and opened the Scriptures to us?" [33]They got up and returned at once to Jerusalem. There they found the Eleven and those with them, assembled together [34]and saying, "It is true! The Lord has risen and has appeared to Simon." [35]Then the two told what had happened on the way, and how Jesus was recognized by them when he broke the bread.*

We see, as these young men repented and believed, that they "got up and returned at once to Jerusalem." They did this because that's where they knew they would find a community of people with whom they could process this amazing discovery.

We have found that, at the point of connection with Jesus, the community we have worked so hard to build becomes a powerhouse of discipleship in which young people can process what God is doing in their lives. In my experience, the moment where a young person meets with God is often a really powerful experience that needs to be processed quickly before the enemy attempts to steal the seed that has been planted. I suggest to all of our leaders that when a young person makes a response to Jesus, the leader needs to follow up with a phone call and a meet-up within a couple of days to begin processing what God has done.

I've also found that it's best to allow the spiritual atmosphere of the whole Target to increase by bringing the salvation story to the whole community, whether they all responded or not. This is best done by sharing testimony of what God has done in the Target. Baptizing the young people and inviting everyone else in the Target to come is one of the best and most powerful ways we've found to do this. Some of my best moments in youth work have been dunking a young person, with the wider church cheering, and a bunch of their mates sitting on the front row with a mixture of hunger, awe, and fear plastered across their faces. Ideally, I get the young people to share their own story at some point, but if they're not ready, then sometimes I will do it for them.

When people meet Jesus, often we'll start small groups attached to the Target. We usually do this just before the main Target gathering so that new Christians can invite others into the process and see how it remains clearly connected. In these small groups, we run through the basics of faith and discuss what things they want to investigate. Even if the Target is small enough and most have come to faith, it's still often best to take the extra time before or after the main Target because the principle of keeping the commonality of the community still applies. We try and resist totally changing the structure of what we've been doing in the Target, but rather seek to make space for people to share the testimony of what God has done and give thanks for it. Keeping the commonality helps as we move forward to multiplication in the commission phase, which we'll get to in the next chapter.

The Circle

The tool we use to help young people process what has happened in their lives is the circle. We don't necessarily have to teach this to our young people (although this can be really useful), but we always run through this

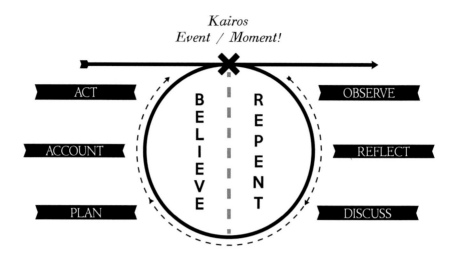

Kairos
Event / Moment!

ACT — OBSERVE

BELIEVE | REPENT

ACCOUNT — REFLECT

PLAN — DISCUSS

process with them to help give the seed good ground in which to grow. The circle is an easy way of encouraging young people to process what God has done in their lives.[13]

The arrow represents their lives. In all of our lives, we have events or moments in time that challenge us to learn or change. The Greek word for these moments in time is Kairos. The challenge is to keep this Kairos moment from slipping away before it successfully changes our lives as we thought it would. The young people in our Targets will have these Kairos moments constantly, but none is more powerful that connecting with Jesus for the first time. Let's take a moment to consider how we try and effectively lead our young people to process this amazing Kairos and actually act upon it for the rest of their lives.

Have you ever watched the early rounds of *X-Factor*, *American Idol* or a similar talent show? I love these kinds of shows. One of my favorite bits is when people with no musical talent whatsoever put themselves in front of the world to display their lack of ability to sing. Simon Cowell sits behind his desk and hits them with one of his famous lines. My favorite example happened on an *American Idol* show when he was listening to a young lady called Jay.

....

[13] If you choose to teach the Circle to students, *Target — Lifeshapes for Teenagers* will be a helpful resource.

Simon: *I've got to stop this. It is so way off — WAY off Mariah Carey. It wasn't why I was laughing but...*

Jay: *My voice is strong. I need help.*

Simon: *You do. You need a helpline.*

We all love the part of the shows when these poor people have this crushing moment and they realize that Simon doesn't think they can sing as well as they thought they could. The people who really amaze and confuse me are the ones that go back year after year. They say, "Well Simon, this is my ninth attempt to prove to you that I can sing," only to be crushed yet again. The question is why on earth these people don't learn. They can't sing, and they need to find something else to have a go at.

While it's amusing to watch these wonderful crash-and-burn moments, I sometimes wonder if God feels the same about us at times. I picture Him wondering why on earth these people don't learn. The circle is all about helping the young people learn from the experiences they have so that God can mold and shape them like clay in a potter's hands.

Observe

Observation is simply discovering what happened. If we take young people to an event and we're not sure what God has done, then we need to ask them. We always suggest that our leaders take the time to talk to the young people we're working with to find out what's going on in their lives. This is especially important when God has had a chance to do something. I'm normally flabbergasted about what God is actually doing in the lives of the young people I know. All it takes is asking to find out what it is and help them go on a discipleship journey. Our job as leaders at this point is to simply discover what it is that young people have discovered.

Sometimes I've found that young people have very little idea, and all they'll be able to say is that they've connected with "something." That's fine at this point. I simply look to affirm what they have experienced and tell them that it's normal but that it's a good idea for us to get more of a chance to talk it through and explore it properly.

Reflect

The reflect process is a chance for us to help them think, debate, and work out what has happened. The key to this isn't jumping straight into telling them but to go on a journey. I try and get young people to ask me questions about it. I always make sure to constantly point them to Jesus. This point in the discussion is the place to start working in some of the learning points of why we can meet with God. For example, I'll often say, "We can meet with God because of what Jesus did on the cross." This is the chance to start to explain to them what has happened. Even the Apostle Paul wasn't sure what on earth was going on when he met with Jesus on his life journey. God had to send a believer to pray for him and help him process what was going on. We have the privilege of being the people whom God sends to these young people to help the scales start falling from the eyes of their understanding.

Discuss

Young people need peers with whom they can work out their faith. Whenever possible, get all the young people who have met with God together, and get them to discuss it. That's the point of our Truth Revolution DVD resource—to take the young people through a process in which they can discuss all the key issues of Christianity. It is specifically designed with new believers and searching young people in mind.

It's important that the young people get a chance to discuss with others what has happened and look at some of the key theology to understand what has happened. Jesus took the time on the Emmaus road to discuss with the men He met and to help them work out what their experiences meant. Likewise, we have found that the process of taking time to help young people work out their faith is vital. Often, people get excited about the stories of lives being changed and salvation moments at events and forget that this part of the young person's journey is one of the most vital and yet often hidden sacred moments.

Plan

James tells us that faith without deeds is dead. Faith is to be lived out, and young people need to embrace the idea of living out their faith. The best way to help them do this is to help them come up with a plan. We get young people to consider how they will engage in the three areas of the triangle:

UP — How will they learn to pray and read the Bible?

IN — How will they now relate to the Target community? Who will be their key peers and their mentor?

OUT — Who (in or out of the Target) would they like to see come to faith?

Get them to make these plans a real TARGET:

✖ Testing: Make it something that will push you so that you'll be sure to move forward.

✖ Achievable: Make it something that you can actually do. Don't make it so hard that you'll never make it.

✖ Real: Make a specific plan. What are the real steps that you will actually take?

✖ God-given: Make it a plan that you give totally to God. Make sure it fits with His teachings.

✖ Enabling: Make it something that you do yourself, not something that someone else should do.

✖ Time-specific: Make a schedule with a beginning and an end.

Using this simple tool, I help young people make plans that they will actually do and that they actually have a chance of sticking to. The key is to try and keep their plans simple enough so that they can achieve them and so that you can alsohelp make sure that they do.

Account

The key to winning the battle and actually acting upon the plans that young people make is accountability. This can usually be done within a small group. I always make a list of the plans and get young people to give feedback on how they are doing each time I see them. Creating this accountability process sets young people up well for the rest of their walk with Jesus as they journey through life. I've found that the ones who do it effectively from the beginning always grow the fastest. I wish someone had explained this process to me when I was a young teenager trying to work out my vibrant faith in Jesus but making unsustainable plans without any accountability that I never believed I could actually keep.

Act

Get on with it.

I've found that young people are generally exceedingly good at observing, reflecting, and discussing and usually hopeless at planning, accountability, and action. Getting them to act upon their newfound faith is the key to making good disciples. The accountability process is obviously important.

I've also found it really helpful to emphasize the importance of living a life of adventure with Jesus. Sharing the adventures that I am currently going on with young people helps to draw action from them because they also want to go on an adventure with the Father and act upon the things that God is saying to them. Again, if they learn how to actually live out their faith and live out the things that God is saying at this early stage, then we're setting them up to be world changers throughout their lives, simply by living out and acting on the things that God is doing within them.

Up, In, and Out in the connection phase

Let's take a moment to see how our leaders have effectively operated in all the elements of the triangle at the connection stage of our Targets.

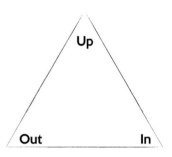

UP — embracing God

This phase is where we really go for it in terms of getting the young people to embrace God. This is usually a risk, and we've found the desperate need to make sure we smother the process in prayer. When we did the first-ever Glory Revolution gospel event, we had an intercession team crying out to God constantly for the young people from 9 a.m. until the event finished at 11 p.m. We held the event in a nightclub in the center of town, so the sound engineers were slightly surprised by all these prayer warriors calling out to Jesus all day. I think we might have made an impression!

I've found that we really need to remember that God wants this to work much more than we do. For years, I was under the impression that I had to convince God to move in the lives of young people. What utter rubbish!

God loves young people much more than I ever could, and therefore He is desperate to have the opportunity to work in their lives and change them by his power if we will get out of the way enough for Him to act. When we act as though that's true, then we find we operate with more faith and much more confidence in sharing the Good News.

We also presume that something has actually happened when we get around to asking the young people what has happened and help them process the Kairos. The one thing I say to our leaders at the point where they have a Target ready for connection is go for it, and I make sure that they and their team are praying lots.

IN — embracing one another

The focus of the IN during the connection phase needs to be the discipleship of those who want to be discipled. I have had countless meetings with leaders and told them that they need to spend less time with the young people who aren't interested in really processing the Kairos because it's a sacrifice worth making. We try to remember that Jesus only did what He saw the Father doing, so at this stage, we need to look for what we see the Father doing and proactively engage with that as the highest priority in order to enable the young people who are meeting with Jesus to process what has happened.

The key we've found at this point in a Target is to allow the depth of community to really develop, even if you lose a few of the fringe young people. I always find this a hard process because, ideally, I want to keep hold of all the young people. But, I find that you simply have to prioritize the young people who are people of peace and who actually want discipleship. Jesus often allowed people to walk away from Him. Think about the rich young ruler who came to Jesus in Mark 10:21-22:

> [21]*Jesus looked at him and loved him. "One thing you lack," he said. "Go, sell everything you have and give to the poor, and you will have treasure in heaven. Then come, follow me."*
> [22]*At this the man's face fell. He went away sad, because he had great wealth.*

When Jesus saw that this young man's face fell, He didn't chase after him trying to make the message easier. Jesus simply allowed the young man to leave and focused on those (His disciples) who were prepared to give things up to follow Him. Since we have limited capacity, we simply are forced to focus on those who actually want to be discipled. When we have very successfully built a strong community, we find that often the young people who aren't ready actually stay around anyway, even if they disappear for a few weeks.

As an overall leader, I have to get my team to be proactive in the right places at the right times, and, after the *kairos* of salvation, the priority must be discipling these young people.

OUT — embracing the lost

The OUT in the connection phase is getting young people to hear and engage with the message of Good News that will change their lives. We decided a long time ago that it's better to take the risk and not look back, knowing that it's God's responsibility to change a life, not ours.

It's good to remember that watching God change lives is one of the greatest privileges of our lives. I often share with the wider church what God has been doing and the amazing wonder of how He has grabbed hold of another life and flipped it on its head. It was a joy last year to see more than 100 young people across all of our Targets give their lives to Jesus in a multitude of different ways. God doesn't have a simple formula, so we find that we constantly have to be aware that Jesus is moving and look for the signs of what He is up to in our Targets. We have to become experts at watching for the signs of the Kingdom breaking out, and when it does, we have to do our best to protect what God is doing and help the young people work out what's going on.

CHAPTER 6

PHASE 4—
COMMISSION

'We're done!" we said to each other. Young people were coming into the Kingdom, and they were being effectively discipled. So the job was done, right?

The problem was that God had other ideas. We had more than 200 teenagers in our Targets, and a lot of them were giving their lives to Jesus. But, there was still a nagging thought in my mind: How did we make this begin to multiply? The Bible seemed to talk about multiplication growth being what's expected in the Kingdom, and yet we were trying to develop these Targets one by one. We realized that we needed a way to get these Targets to multiply.

Jesus didn't say He was finished at this point with His disciples, after all. Lots of them had given their lives to follow Him and were being discipled, but then Jesus did something very interesting: He left them. And He left them with a challenge—a command.

Matthew 28:19-20
[19]Therefore go and make disciples of all nations, baptizing them in the name of the Father and of the Son and of the Holy Spirit, [20]and teaching them to obey everything I have commanded you. And surely I am with you always, to the very end of the age.

So many youth groups out there are trying desperately to "protect" their young people from the big, bad world. While I understand the heart behind this idea, I have seen it create droves of young people living double lives. One of these lives is a lovely Christian persona that knows all the right answers. The other one usually comes out to play with their non-Christian friends. The two can look completely different. I get asked by lots of youth workers how to break this double life. We've discovered through a process of trying to find a multiplication model that the answer is simple— commission them!

I had been a youth worker for nearly seven years and had been trying to tackle this double-life issue with every single one of the young people before I discovered that I would never be able to teach our young people to break the cycle of living a double life. As I thought about it, I started to realize that the only young people I knew who didn't lead a double life were ones who had allowed their two worlds to collide. To do this, the young people needed to be in Targets with their non-Christian friends. I firmly believe that there is no better time to do this than as soon as they make a connection with Jesus.

You have to trust me when I say that commissioning young people for mission is the best discipleship tool I've found.

Connecting the dots between our desire to get the Targets to multiply and our desire to stop young people from living double lives led us to the solution of giving young people even more responsibility by multiplying the Targets they were in and by commissioning them to live a radical life for Jesus. Sometimes a Target will multiply into two, and sometimes it will be able to multiply into lots of variations from the original Target. But no matter what multiplication looks like, we always ask a key question: How can young people lead their friends on the same process that they have been on?

The Target that had come out of our original centralized youth event had grown significantly and was pushing toward 50 young people. The leaders had seen God do some amazing things, and lots of young people had become Christians. We started to look for ways in which we could see more Targets spawned out of this large Target. From this original group of young people, we had a go at a football-based Target, a similar youth-event-style Target for older young people based in the same area, and one Target based in the local school. Leaders worked alongside young people to run through the same process of making contact, building community, and aiding connection. What we discovered through this exploration process was very interesting: leaders and young people really grasped the vision. The neighborhood Target has grown significantly, the school's Target has multiplied within the school and is now two Targets, and the football-based Target went on a crazy journey. Let me tell you about it.

The football-based Target started with a few young people who hung out with a few leaders and played football in a local park. Today, we have a mini-football league where all the Targets that have multiplied out can play each other in a five-a-side league. Other local churches have caught the bug and have started Targets based on the same model. The leaders who started this original outreach now run regular gathered connection events where they get Christian football players to come and share the gospel with all the young people in their Targets. The multiplication growth in this area has been so explosive that for a while we simply didn't know what to do with it or how to keep it growing without getting in the way. God has breathed His life into these Targets and given us another helpful understanding. Even more, this multiplication has been aided by other churches jumping into the ring to get involved in what God has been doing. From a start of three or four young people, there are now more than 150 young people in these Targets, based at all sorts of churches in Sheffield who are going on this journey from contact to community to connection to commission.

I've learned an awful lot over the last few years, but one of my major humble-pie moments has been over the growth of the football-based Targets. For years, I had been loudly telling anyone who would listen that Targets needed to be geographically based due to the fact that teenagers' lives are very geographically based. This came out of the original light-bulb moment that had started our journey toward having multiple communities. But what we discovered with the growth of the football Targets was that this method isn't restricted to being neighborhood focused. The football Targets draw young people from all over the city. Often the young people club together into Targets from certain areas of the city, but we discovered in this multiplication phase of our youth work that Targets can be made up of a network of young people.

Now we understand that our Targets can be either neighborhood or network-focused. A vast majority of our Targets are still geographically based within a local neighborhood. But, we have been experimenting more and more on how we can learn to work within the existing networks that young people already have to plant and multiply Targets that reach the lost young people of Sheffield.

Over the last year and a half, as we've encouraged all of our leaders to consider how we multiply our Targets, we have seen growth from 200 to 650 young people being plugged into Targets, with another 150 on the edges through early contact work based around detached approaches. This has further increased the messy nature of our youth work, but we've also seen more and more young people giving their lives to Jesus.

We shouldn't be surprised—multiplication is biblical.

> ### Acts 2:42-47
> [42]*They devoted themselves to the apostles' teaching and to the fellowship, to the breaking of bread and to prayer.* [43]*Everyone was filled with awe, and many wonders and miraculous signs were done by the apostles.* [44]*All the believers were together and had everything in common.* [45]*Selling their possessions and goods, they gave to anyone as he had need.* [46]*Every day they continued to meet together in the temple courts. They broke bread in their homes and ate together with glad and sincere hearts,* [47]*praising God and enjoying the favor of all the people. And the Lord added to their number daily those who were being saved.*

One of the main options we've explored to see this multiplication of our Targets is encouraging young people to consider if they have a vision for a method of creating contact with other young people. Basically, they start the journey all over again. Usually, the vision for this Target revolves around the vision of the original one. We've found that often they'll stay in the same geographical area, or use the same sport, or the same music, etc.

As a team, we started to love the idea of making things that could be effectively commissioned to multiply. In order for things to be multipliable, we try and always come up with Targets that are lightweight enough and flexible enough so that other leaders or young people can take on the ideas.

To help us do this, we have a lens through which we try and look at our Targets. We call this the M&M lens. We imagine that we are looking at our Targets through a pair of spectacles. In the left lens, we place the word 'missional.' We ask ourselves the question: Is it still reaching the lost? In the right lens, we place the word 'multipliable.' In other words, is it replicable? In order for our Targets to get to the commissioning phase, they needed to be multipliable.

With this in mind, we changed the way we saw the size of a Target. We became much stricter on forcing leaders to consider multiplying the Target when it got to 30 young people. I had realized through all my years of leading youth work that most people could manage to lead a group of under 30 teenagers. Teenagers themselves could cope with this number, and an average church volunteer with little training could manage this number. But beyond the threshold of 30, only good youth workers could keep the Target moving, and the larger the group, the higher the level of professionalism required. Although we wanted to have good youth work at a high quality, we noticed as we looked through our multipliable lens that continuing to hire professional youth workers when Targets hit 40–50 young people was simply not sustainable. We were totally unable to keep increasing our budget sufficiently to grow in this manner. The only way to proceed was to keep multiplying the Targets so that they didn't get over the 30-person threshold. This has required huge discipline because sometimes it feels like the Target is just starting to fly when we have to start considering what it will mean to multiply it.

Training leaders and young people

"Our leaders are totally unsupported," one of my staff members said one morning as we were chatting about how the youth work was going. We had grown really large by this point, and our youth work was probably the biggest church-based youth work in the country. I was about to leap into defending the way in which we were doing it when I realized that she was spot on. We had focused so much in the past few years on pushing everyone out from the center and fighting our desire to control everything that we had allowed our leaders to be completely unsupported, untrained, and left to their own devices. We had set up some online systems that enabled us to comply with child-protection rules by having people fill out all the forms that they needed, but this wasn't helping leaders to learn and grow. We were also quickly becoming a vast and disparate group of people who didn't feel sufficiently connected to the church. We had a problem!

We agonized as a team for a while about running training nights. "People won't come," said Dan. He was right, and I knew it. If we put on regular training at the church, the leaders simply wouldn't come. We'd never get a subject that would work for everyone, so busy people would be getting busier without reason.

Finally, running this question through the missional and multipliable lenses quickly showed us we were barking up the wrong tree. As we brainstormed, we talked about training that we had found helpful for us as a staff team, and this gave us a sliver of an idea. The senior leaders of our church gathered key leaders every six months for a training weekend in which we were taken through an evaluation process of the area of ministry that we led. This was helpful because we personalized any teaching we heard to the youth ministry and then came up with a series of goals for the next six months. We gave these goals to the senior leaders, who asked us how they had gone six months later. We had come up with some of our best ideas and revelations in this forum and had instigated real change.

Pippa mused thoughtfully, "A Forge leaders weekend…" We began batting around the idea of running a Forge-wide weekend every six months for everyone that ran a Target. We knew we needed to gather more than 100 leaders together and that the training would need to be good or else they wouldn't come the next time. Dan said, "I think a weekend is too long," as we were looking at what we would try and pack into the weekend. I objected, "Too long? But how do we get through everything?" Again, however, I had that sinking feeling of knowing that he was spot on. Asking for a whole weekend from our volunteer Target leaders was an awful lot on top of everything they were doing leading the Targets themselves. Pippa suggested that we try and get it down to a day, so we did. We compressed the teaching down to a minimum and worked on exercises that would help the Target leaders work out where they were in terms of the four C phases outlined in this book and also how to move forward.

These leader training days are now a massive highlight of my year. Every six months, all of our Target leaders gather to look at where they are, to dream of what God might do, and to make some concrete plans for the next six months. We always get them to share a little with each other so that the whole team feels connected with what's going on and so that we can share in each other's successes and help each other in our struggles. This approach has also enabled us to start distributing the shared learning happening in Targets across the entire Forge Youth network. We have now joined this training approach with all of our Forge kids' teams as they have launched into a Targets method. As one person learns, we all learn. It's really exciting to hear someone share a revelation that they've had and notice a load of people grab him or her over coffee to find out how that person did it so that they can all replicate it in their Target. It's been really fulfilling to gather the teams of leaders who are the real heroes of Forge Youth together in one place. My mind constantly boggles as I hear the countless stories of God breaking in and changing some of the most challenging lives.

The last idea we discovered in encouraging Targets to get to this point of commission was to start training events at the church to help the young people grow in their leadership skills so that they feel equipped to lead a Target, whether alongside some friends or with an adult leader. This year, we started a training program that we call 'Redefine' with the tagline, *"Be Redefined, Go Redefine!"* Young people commit to coming for a year, and we keep the cost at a minimum so that teenagers from all backgrounds can come. We train them for three weekends spread through the year with deep teaching, great worship, and discussion groups that help them use the Kairos circle to mine out the vision that God has given them to reach their friends.

I was chatting with one of our young people who excitedly told me how she had become a Christian at Redefine. Some of our young people were so passionate about being trained for God's call that they had invited their non-Christian friend who they thought was close. At first, I was a little unsure about this, because Redefine is clearly a high-bar leadership training weekend. But she gave her life to Jesus on the first night and is now one of the most sold-out young leaders we have. I'm guessing that giving her life to Jesus in the context of high-bar challenge made sure she started on the right foot. Hilariously, at the second training weekend of the year, she came again and dragged along her twin sister, who then did exactly the same thing. They are now two amazing women of God who are part of reaching out to their whole friendship group, and they have an incredible vision for God transforming their school.

These experiences led me to consider the place of the church building within youth work. Increasingly, very few of our Targets actually meet in the church building itself. They all meet out where young people would naturally already congregate because it's much easier to do the contact phase of a Target there. We now see our central buildings through the M&M lens too and use them in a way that will enable our Targets to be more missional and that will help them multiply. If it doesn't encourage M&M, then we just don't do it.

One example among many of how we used the M&M lens to make a very tough call for Forge was with our weekend away. For my first seven years of youth work, I had run a weekend away called Time Out for all our young people. These weekends had been fantastic times of seeing young people grow and develop quickly and seeing others come to faith. I had drummed into our youth team over the years how important it was for us to have the weekend away, because it was one of the few times when we gathered a large number of our Targets and young people together.

As Forge began to grow and grow, these weekends became bigger logistical challenges for us to organize and became financially tricky. Lots of our young people weren't from well-to-do backgrounds, so we had to raise most of the costs to subsidize the young people. One week before our biggest ever weekend away, I had an awful realization. More than 200 of us were heading off for what promised to be an amazing weekend, but the weekend was failing one of our key filters. It was missional, but it certainly wasn't multipliable.

My team and I had raised more than 20,000 pounds[14] in order to take all of the young people, and it had taken a vast amount of work and organization to make that happen. On top of that, making a program work for young people from such varied and different backgrounds was a total nightmare. It really wasn't a multipliable strategy to reach a city with 66,000 teenagers. There was nothing that worked for everyone.

I decided that if we were going to reach our whole city, then growing a weekend away for all of our young people simply wasn't going to work. I kept my mouth shut, and we ran what was to be our very last Forge-wide weekend away. It was fantastic; lots of young people came to faith, and we saw many young people grow in their walk with Jesus. Although I had many wobbles about the decision, I gathered my team just after the weekend and confessed that we were ignoring our very own filter—and that was why I was cancelling the next weekend. There was a little sadness in the room, but the overwhelming sense was that it was like lifting a massive burden off their shoulders. The truth was that it was killing us trying to organize such a huge undertaking while trying to do all the youth work we were running. We didn't have many staff members to make it happen, and the weight of burden was too much for us.

....

[14] That's well over $30,000 for you Americans.

The next year we ran seven much smaller weekends away with individual Target leaders getting together with a couple of similar Targets to run a weekend. The result was that it was much easier to organize, much cheaper, plus we had found a strategy for reaching a whole city.

We have learned that unless we keep viewing everything we do through the M&M filter, we start to go off track. Things can be seemingly brilliant, fruitful, and successful but fail this important test. Now we make sure that all of our events, organization, and Targets are designed to serve the mission and to be multipliable.

"What about worship services?" an incredulous youth worker asked, as I met him and I shared what God had been up to in Sheffield amongst our awesome young people. I explained my experience of trying to run worship services for young people and told him I didn't much fancy it. He said, "Oh, but aren't they missing out on something?" I wanted to hit him! He was supposed to be excited about what God was doing, not point out all of the problems. Most of my frustration was because I had that familiar sinking feeling that he was right. I remembered how as a teenager I enjoyed going to worship and teaching services.

Coincidentally, my key leader Dan came to see me a few weeks later with the vision of starting a worshipping and teaching night to gather a few of the Targets that he oversaw. It felt like God was stirring something, so we decided to give it a try, and rather than making it just for a couple of Targets, we threw it open wide for anyone who wanted to come. We talked long and hard about whether it went against our M&M principle. The only way I was happy with it was when we decided to only do it once every other month. Someone came up with the name Alive, and we started having a go.

Today, we have an amazing Forge youth band and a great gathering point for any of our young people from across all of our Targets who fancy it. We've found that keeping it every other month has held momentum. Moreover, belonging in the Targets has actually helped us give some deeper teaching, provide some great worship, and do prayer ministry in a way that is impossible with just a few teenagers in a Target. We've found we've got an awful lot still to learn about how to run major youth services, but it feels like the right journey to be on, so long as we never lose the passion of planting multiple, multipliable, missional communities of youth through Targets.

It's a simple answer to a complicated question: How do we reach a generation with the Good News of Jesus **with multiple, multipliable, missional Targets?**

What if we're stuck? The time for earthquakes

An earthquake happens when two plates in the crust of the earth become stuck together over a period of time and then, after tension has built up within the earth, they suddenly slip a long way. This causes violent shaking of the earth, but it also causes the plates to get back on track. Youth work is one of the areas of ministry and outreach that is most likely to get stuck. I and other leaders have often become aware that we've gotten stuck at one of these points on the Target, and we can't quite work out how to move forward without causing some problems amongst our young people or their parents. Sometimes we've built a Target where we've made fantastic contact with loads of young people, but we can't see how to move to community without losing a few. Lots of times we've gotten stuck with a great community where the gospel just doesn't seem to be breaking through. Our most common mistake, which is by far the hardest to spot, is when we've gone through all the phases and seen young people connecting with Jesus, but we haven't seen them commissioned to multiply the Target. I've found that the process of gathering our leaders together every six months has helped us spot this sticking earlier, but the question still remains: How do we move forward without causing some sort of earthquake in the group?

The answer we've found is that you can't. Instead, it's time to strap in and have an earthquake!

In my experience, an earthquake is the only way forward. I'm not saying that I proactively look for trouble, but I have been known to go for a shock factor to provoke us to the next stage of the Target. At the end of the day, any Target that is doing some of the 4 Cs but hasn't moved on to the next phase is not living out the full promise of what God wants to do. It's easy to sit back on our laurels whenever we see the next bit of breakthrough and pat ourselves on the back at how well we've done instead of moving on to the next phase.

I love the TV show *The West Wing*. The viewer gets drawn into the drama of all the crazy decisions and situations that the president of the United States has to deal with every day. Almost always, once the latest disaster is averted or international crisis is fixed, the president turns to his senior staff and says, "What's next?" They then move on with the next item on the agenda. I've found that it's so important not to stop at any phase. As we see the next piece of breakthrough in our Target, we have to look around the team and ask what's next.

We once had two very small Targets of Christian young people who were having a wonderful time meeting together and meeting with God. They had community and connection but no commission and therefore no real contact with their friends. This led to the age-old problem of lots of the young people living double lives. The only way I could change the situation was to unleash an earthquake. I stopped both groups, gathered them together, and told them we were going to do activities that were about outreach. I started traipsing them around the local area and praying for it. They hated it at first. But eventually, they began to get a heart for it, and we put on a coffee shop hangout where we all hung out and got some of their school friends to come. The whole process went on from there. Amazingly, we lost very few young people in this process, and through it we made real disciples rather than a holy huddle trying to hide from the world and actually falling into its traps.

If we have young people who are stuck, we usually suggest that our teams see how stuck they are by starting with the gentle approach. If this doesn't work, then we presume that we're stuck and the only way forward is throwing them straight into the depths of whatever it is they need. I've found that this usually works, although I always get the team to do some serious praying if we need to do it. The key to having an earthquake with a bunch of young people is to make sure we get the team on board. If the team isn't on board, then the earthquake ends up as a disaster. One of the lessons I've learned is that if the team itself is stuck and doesn't want to move forward, then the first place of battle is with the leadership team rather than with the teenagers. Often I'll try and do something that will provoke an earthquake amongst the team first before discerning whether an earthquake with the young people is required.

Up, In, and Out in the commission phase

UP — embracing God

Engaging young people in deep discipleship is vital as you commission them. They need to gain depth in their relationship as they step out. The key to them engaging in real discipleship is for what they are learning to have practical outworking that keeps it real. In all our discipleship, we seek not only to encourage the young people but also to challenge them about what they are actually going to do about it.

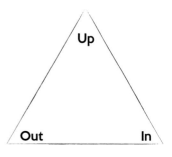

When we run the Redefine training weekends, we always get the young people to leave the weekend with a three-month plan of how they are going to mine deeper into their relationship with Jesus. Sometimes these plans are simply amazing. I've listened to young people taking some serious challenges in terms of Bible reading, prayer, solitude, and more into their everyday lives with the support of their friends.

We have to encourage young people to go deep with Jesus. I've become sick of the idea that the way to do this is to spoon-feed young people with information. Information never changes lives; revelation does! Revelation comes by giving the young people tools, encouragement, and challenge to mine into Jesus for themselves. Our goals should be to enable even the least educated young people to access the Bible for themselves, to pray, to hear from God, and to learn His ways. They do this by watching the lives of those who are further along the journey and then chasing after Jesus for themselves using the tools that they are taught on the way.

IN — embracing one another

We've found that the temptation in the commission phase is to close the loop of the community. However, it's really important to continue to press forward the depth of relationships that have been made without creating a Christian bubble for them. The reason this is important is that discipleship isn't done in the classroom; it's done through life. Young people can't simply learn information; they need to live it.

Vibrant community amongst Christian peers is what most young people point to as the thing that most helps them stay connected to God and to church. We mustn't just get the young people fired up with vision and then send them out on their own like lambs to the slaughter. This is why we always get our young people to work together in community on any vision that they want to implement. Usually, they work alongside some adult leaders too. The depth of relationships is what enables the continuation of multiplication, so rather than being less important in this phase, it's actually more important.

OUT — embracing the lost

We have to go back to the start of the Targets' journey as we commission the Targets and look to how we are going to make contact with the next wave of young people. It's time to ask the question yet again: How do we make contact with a generation that has lost touch with the church? Getting the young people to drive the vision makes this process easy. Our youth ministry may be making contact with more than 800 young people every week, but there are still another 65,000 remaining in Sheffield. This is a sobering thought to us at Forge and makes us realize that we need M&M (missional and multipliable) Targets more than ever before.

Whenever we get into congratulating ourselves on the size of our youth group and the wonderful stories where we've seen God do miraculous things, we try and remind ourselves of the size of the task ahead. Just as God said to Gideon in Judges 7:2:

> The LORD said to Gideon, "You have too many men. I cannot deliver Midian into their hands, or Israel would boast against me, 'My own strength has saved me.'"

We know that we constantly have to remember that the task ahead of us is impossible. We are incapable of fighting the battle without God breathing His breath into what we're doing. All we're trying to do is learn as best we can from everything that He's done so that we minimize the number of mistakes we make that get in the way of what God is doing. We know that God wants to reach every single young person of Sheffield, and we know that the best way to see more of His Kingdom breaking out is to simply try and learn everything we can from what He's been doing, lay our lives down every day, and pray like crazy.

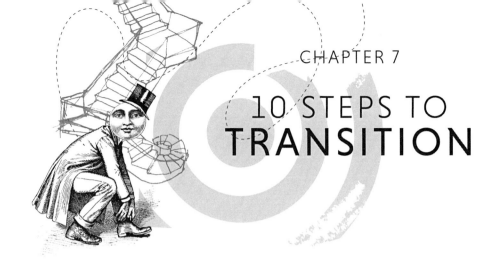

CHAPTER 7

10 STEPS TO TRANSITION

We have been blessed to watch God transform our youth ministry over the last three years so that it reaches many young people. If you've been inspired by the idea of missional communities of youth as you've read this book, this section is designed to help you make that a reality in your context. I'll mine out from all of our mistakes and successes the process that I use to get your youth work running on these principles. These stages should help you whether you lead a megachurch of thousands looking to impact a whole nation, or a small local church with a few young people hoping to reach a neighborhood, or even if you are a concerned individual who has noticed a few young people hanging out in the local park, and you want to see them receive the hope of the gospel of Jesus.

At the end of the chapter, I've included a timeline that should help you put these steps into action in a manner that will allow you to transition your youth work to work on a Targets (missional community) model and be at the point of seriously multiplying within two years.

Step 1: Take stock

The first step of the journey is to take stock of what you have. Try and get as close as you can to the raw, brutal facts. The better sense you get of what young people you actually have, where they belong, and how they are being discipled, the easier you'll find it will be to do the following steps. This section includes a number of exercises that we find helpful in examining the youth work we're running. They should help you in your stock-taking process.

The best way to do this is not in isolation as a youth worker or as a church leader sitting in an office. Instead, you will want to give these exercises out to a number of people who are involved in the youth work or who have some sort of vested interest, such as parents, and then gather everyone together and compare the answers. Look at where you all agree and where you have differing scores or ideas. Take some time to discuss why you've come up with something different and try and get as accurate a look at the youth ministry as possible.

The following table helps us look at the numbers of young people and the numbers of groups. As you fill it in, don't just write the raw numbers. Also add the comments, thoughts, and ideas that hit you as you write down the bare facts. As much as possible, try not to guess at these figures. Get them as accurate as possible. Also, be really careful not to count the same young people 30 times just because they are attending more than one program.

❯ THE FACTS TABLE ❮

QUESTION	ANSWER
How many young people do you see across your programs each week?	
How many young people do you know overall?	
How many young people belong to a smaller community (small group, Target, etc)?	
How many different groups / communities / outreach programs do you have?	
How many adult leaders do you have?	
How many young people are in leadership positions?	
How many young people are wholeheartedly committed to your ministry?	

After doing this exercise, it might be worth taking a moment to note the key thoughts that jump out at you. Take a moment to cross-reference the numbers of young people with the numbers of groups and the numbers of leaders. Note how much overlap you have between young people attending multiple groups as this requires extra leaders and/or creates very tired leaders.

The SWOT Analysis

The next exercise will help you look at the strengths, weaknesses, opportunities, and threats in your youth work. Fill in the four quadrants as you think about your youth work as a whole. If you have a large youth work, then consider the mega-themes that span across the whole thing rather than digging in too much into individual communities.

Strengths

Consider what things you feel that you do well. It might be a particular program or you may feel that you create great resources. Do you feel like you train and equip leaders well? Are you reaching lots of lost teenagers? Do you have strong discipleship?

Opportunities

Think about where young people remain untouched by the church. Maybe there is a place where lots of them hang out, a neighborhood that doesn't have a church, a school with some of your young people, a need for sports teams but not enough coaches, etc. You should be able to think of all sorts of opportunities that have remained untapped. There are always so many more.

Weaknesses

What are the main weaknesses of what you are running? Be brutally honest. We all make mistakes, have blind spots, and end up with weaknesses. The worst thing you can do is bury your head in the sand and pretend that you don't have any shortcomings. Think it through and try and work out what you should be doing better. It could be anything from raising and training leaders to telling young people about Jesus.

Threats

What things threaten to prevent you from moving forward into the future? What might slow you down or even make it impossible to move? Again, be really honest and don't hold anything back. It could be anything from a church council that wants everything to remain the same to a youth team that just doesn't want to follow you in the direction you want to go to having no money to get yourself going.

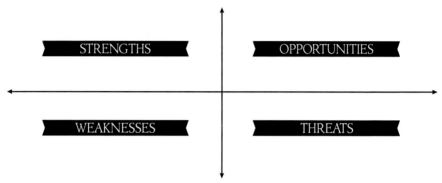

The 4 Cs

The final exercise we'll do in this section is an exercise that we get our Target leaders to do for their Targets all the time. It's designed to help them work out where they are in the 4 Cs process and therefore see how they need to be operating at any given time. We're going to use the exercise here to consider the big picture of your youth work and how it's going.

On each axis is one of the 4 C words (contact, community, connection, and commission), with little marks all the way up each axis. Mark your youth work on a scale from 1 to 10 for each of the different Cs. Here are a couple of thoughts to help you.

Contact

On this axis, take time to consider how well you are making contact with new young people. Focus particularly on reaching young people who don't yet know Jesus. Consider how many new people you have met in the last couple of months, the number of outreach-focused activities or groups you have, and the success of these initiatives or programs. Don't worry too much about how well you are discipling the young people at this stage; simply focus on how well you are making contact with them. Also, think about how well you feel like you understand the young people in the neighborhood within which you work. The better you feel that you know what TV they watch, what films they like, and what music they are into, the higher the score you can give yourself.

Community

Scoring your youth work on this axis is about looking at the three key components of community highlighted in this book: commonality, distinctiveness, and relationship. Think about how much of a sense of commonality there is in your youth work. Do the young people feel like they are a part of something? How distinct are they empowered to feel? Do you have a logo, a brand, a website, a Facebook presence, etc.? Finally and most importantly, how deep do the relationships in your youth work go? Is there depth of sharing between you and the young people, between the leaders and the young people, between the leaders and each other, and between the young people themselves?

Connection

How well are you connecting the young people to Jesus? Take a moment to consider how many young people you've seen give their lives to Jesus this last year. Also consider how many of these young people are still following Jesus and are part of your youth work. This part isn't just about seeing people give their lives to Jesus; also consider how well discipled your young people are and how well your events help create good worship and teaching environments.

Commission

How well are you releasing young people to live their lives and reach their friends? How many of your young people have brought friends along recently? Are the young people active in suggesting how things should be run? Do the young people take active leadership in things within your youth ministry? Have your young people been encouraged to consider how you could work together on reaching their school or neighborhood? The most important question for you to think through here is: Do you have a problem with young people living double lives?

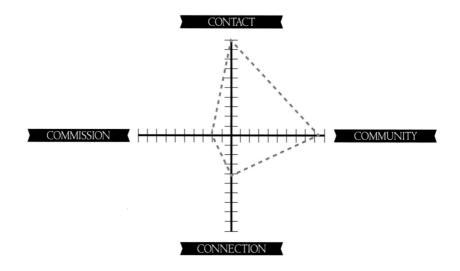

After you mark your scores on the quadrant, we often find it helpful to connect the dots so that what we call the "shape" of your youth work becomes clear. This will give you an overall sense of how well you are doing across the board at these different elements, which will be really helpful when you get to step three and start to work out what your vision should be. We do this process regularly for all of our Targets so that they get a sense of where they are, how they are leading in a particular season, and where they are trying to move.

Step 2: Find some leaders

The second step on your journey is to find a bunch of people who understand what you are trying to do and who will come on board with you for the early stages of the journey. In general, we've found that trying to get everyone on board with an idea that is just an idea is very difficult. Most people will simply look at all the issues that you might have further down the priority list. Instead, at this stage, you need to find a small group of leaders who will commit to the vision of planting the first Targets. You don't even have to tell everyone else what you're doing at this point.

When I first started the journey of planting multiple Targets at St. Thomas in Sheffield, I didn't try to get all of the leaders on board with the idea from day one. I shared the overall vision with the wider team but started by getting a core team of people who were up for the idea. At the time of beginning our first three Targets, the vast majority of our youth team members were operating on a business as usual basis and waiting to hear what was happening in these new outreaches. I gathered my core team of Dan and Pippa to talk about how we were going to go about launching these three new communities. Dan and Pippa then called a small team of committed people to the particular vision of the Targets that they wanted to plant, and we all went from there.

Calling the right people at this stage is absolutely vital. You need people who will help you get these initial Targets going and who will be good at sharing the testimony of what has happened as it unfolds. You also need people who are capable of coping with learning lessons as you go. Dan, Pippa, and I learned so much in our first year of running Targets that has proved invaluable in learning how to crank the handle in multiplication further down the track. If I had picked people who gave up at the first sight of trouble, then we would have all given up a long time ago.

In those early days, we had a mantra that we would try pretty much anything and see what God seemed to bless. When God blessed something, we tried to learn why it was working and look to share that learning between us. Whenever something didn't work, we stopped and tried to work out why it hadn't worked and likewise shared this information. Although in theory this sounds nice and simple, it was often confusing, hard, complicated, and frustrating. You'll need some people with you who are prepared to dig into the trenches with you and go to war through thick and thin. Pippa and Dan certainly did this with me.

On the next page is an exercise to help you think about the people whom you might want to get involved in this early stage of transitioning to run Targets-based youth work. The first thing you have to do is list all the people you can think of (whether they are on your team or not) who you think might be good for this task. Put them in the column on the left. Once you have made your initial list, put a check in each column if that person fits the description at the top of the page. This isn't meant to be an exercise that excludes anyone but simply a way of helping you work out what it is that you think you need at this point. I have deliberately not given any weight to the different characteristics.

NAME							
Has a deep and unshakeable faith							
Has solid accountability							
Is flexible and copes with changes well							
Is very committed to me as a leader							
Has lots of youth experience							
Is easily challengeable							
Is an Apostle, Prophet or Evangelist							
Seems to have caught the vision well							
Is pioneering as a leader by nature							
Is good at sharing testimony							
Has a proven leadership record							

Once you have a list of potential people, then you can choose which ones you ask to come on your first-stage team. Ask these people to come and get involved, and then gather them to share the vision, eat together, and pray. Start to build community with these people because good relationships with them will be vital as you move forward. Don't worry if you don't end up asking a huge number of people to be involved at this stage. Three is a minimum, and I wouldn't suggest any more than 20. You'll struggle to keep the vision pure in its infancy if you have too many people involved. On the other hand, if it's just two of you, then it can be a lonely adventure.

Step 3: Get a vision

The next step is for you as a new little leadership team to come up with a vision for what you are going to do. Sometimes you as a leader may have a strong idea about where you need to start. Still, this step in the process is really important. It's also possible that more than one vision will emerge in this time. When I began with Dan and Pippa, we quickly discovered that we had three very different visions. We managed to gather a sufficient team and therefore decided to go for all three at once. I wouldn't suggest that this is the normal procedure, but it's always worthwhile for a team leader to see what God is saying to other people on your leadership team before bulldozing them with your ideas.

The place to start is by taking some time out to pray and ask God what you are supposed to be doing. It can be really powerful to pray and fast as a team. Get the team to write down any prophetic words or senses that they get. If anyone is drawn to any specific scriptures, then it is worth noting these as well. This process needs to continue throughout the vision creation time. I always find it helpful to buy a specific book in which we write down everything that we've been thinking and hearing from God.

As we were setting the vision on the Lansdown estate, I had the whole team prayer-walking for several months before we met any teenagers at all. In this time, we gathered loads of prophetic words and scriptures as different people in the leadership team heard what they felt like God was saying to us. These words and scriptures were vital in guiding us in the months ahead as we moved forward in making contact with the young people.

You'll need to work out what young people you are trying to make contact with. It may be that you have an obvious target group. When we started in the Lansdown estate, we knew that our goal was to reach the young people living in the two-square-mile block around the neighborhood where we had moved. However, Pippa selected Shiregreen in a much more pragmatic way. She knew that her heart was beating for the inner-city young people of Sheffield. She wanted to work with some of the roughest teenagers of the city, but as we talked about it, there were loads of potential places where she could start. The question was how to narrow the vision for this first Target down to just one of these needy areas. We considered loads of factors in trying to narrow down our search, including where there were very few churches operating (although this was most of the inner-city areas) and where there were clearly lots of young people hanging out on the streets. (Again, this was pretty much every single one of the areas.) The thing that ended up swinging us to this specific area was the fact that Shiregreen had a strong kids' work presence from our church, which meant that we already had contact with a whole load of kids in the area. Some of these kids had now turned into teenagers, and one of our church's adult missional communities had started working with some of them. These were obviously the young people to start with.

As you can see from our early approaches, there isn't one right way to go about finding your vision for your first Target. You can be prophetic, pragmatic, based on relationships, or a mixture of everything. There isn't one right way of going about it, but the key is to properly think and pray through what you are trying to do.

Don't feel like you have to have every detail of your strategy worked out in order to put your vision down on paper. In general, all you really need is a vision for what you are going to do in phase one of your Target and a clear picture of who you are trying to make contact with. Once you've worked this out, you can look at the triangle functions for this phase (mentioned in chapter three) to work out what things should look like as far as activity is concerned.

As I've said, this process often comes easily. If it's proving to be a bit of a struggle, then I would suggest you consider working through the following exercise to help you get a vision. This is a flowchart to help you think through what you already have and how to move forward with what you find. You may want to run through this as a team and use it whenever it is useful for considering what you are doing. I sometimes find that the process of simply seeing it visually helps me to consider the vision a little more clearly.

The Vision Flowchart

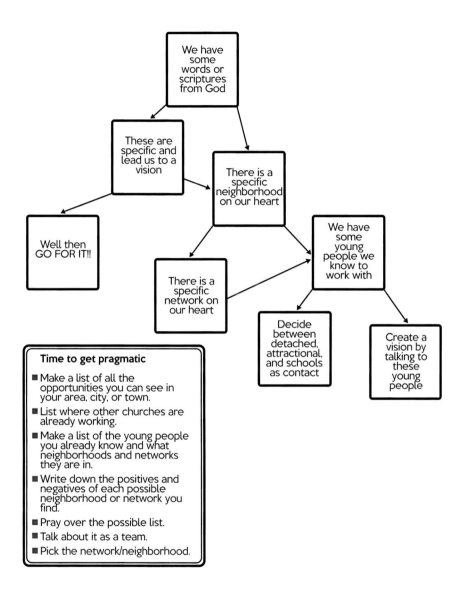

We have some words or scriptures from God

These are specific and lead us to a vision

There is a specific neighborhood on our heart

We have some young people we know to work with

Well then GO FOR IT!!

There is a specific network on our heart

Decide between detached, attractional, and schools as contact

Create a vision by talking to these young people

Time to get pragmatic

- Make a list of all the opportunities you can see in your area, city, or town.
- List where other churches are already working.
- Make a list of the young people you already know and what neighborhoods and networks they are in.
- Write down the positives and negatives of each possible neighborhood or network you find.
- Pray over the possible list.
- Talk about it as a team.
- Pick the network/neighborhood.

Step 4: Launch a pilot

It's now time to start having a go at launching your first Target or Targets. Don't worry if it doesn't feel like the start of something massive. The Bible tells us not to despise the days of small beginnings. When we started our first communities three years ago, we had no idea that God would pour

His blessings on what we were doing or that we'd see more than 10 times multiplication growth. It never feels that exciting when you take your first steps out onto the cold streets, or when you take your first three young people to the zoo. Whatever you have decided to do for your first Target, just remember to start by looking to make contact. Listen to conversations that are happening and become well versed in what the young people are talking about.

One little tip I learned early on in the contact phase of running Targets was to write down as much information as I could immediately after each session, especially when we met new young people. I unfortunately am not blessed with a very good memory, and this is a trait I have discovered is reasonably common among my friends in youth work. Consequently, I have found that vital things like the young people's names will travel straight through my ears and out into the ether without lodging in my brain for more than about 20 minutes. As a team, we always rushed back together after a session where we'd made contact with new young people to pull out our book and write down people's names and any other information we could remember, along with a description of them so that we could remember which one was which the next time. Remembering people's names and important things about them is a powerful way to show that you are trying to build the initial stages of trust and relationship. If you (like me) are not naturally blessed in this area, then you (like me) will just have to work slightly harder at it.

In order to keep the wider church and your wider youth and youth team on your side at this stage in the journey, it's often helpful to refer to this first Target as a pilot. This removes fear and gives people a sense of peace knowing that you and the team are just testing this thing out to see how it goes without jumping too hastily into something for everyone. The language you use will be important because you don't want anybody jumping ship from what you are currently running to join if it's not right for them, just because it sounds like the new and exciting thing. We deliberately waited until our first three Targets had gotten up and running before we started sharing testimony and news from them to inspire people about what was going on.

When we launched our pilot Targets, it felt like nothing happened for the first few months. We mined away and plowed the hard ground. Expect that the initial breakthrough will take a little more work than perhaps you'd like.

If you have started more than one Target at once in this pilot step, then you will find it helpful to meet regularly as Target leaders so that you can share what you're learning, to encourage each other, and to pray for one another. This helps you to avoid multiplying mistakes and helps you multiply successes.

In short, this step is about hopping out of the boat and having a go. You need to trust that you're onto the right thing and that Jesus will do the hard work and bless what you are doing as you step out in faith. I find it helpful to remind the team regularly at these early stages that God wants to see breakthrough way more than we do—and we want to see it pretty badly!

Step 5: Share the testimony

Step five sounds like a very simple step, but we have actually found it to be the key pivot that enables you to develop your youth work from having just a couple of good Targets to enabling a whole movement of multiplying Targets to get off the ground, thus mobilizing a large number of people.

In step two, I suggested that the large majority of people don't catch a vision from an abstract suggestion. This is because the large majority of people need something more concrete to stand on before they start to trust a vision and are ready to give time, effort, and money toward it. This is where effectively sharing of testimony from your initial Targets comes in. Don't worry—you won't need to have stories of hundreds giving their lives to Jesus to convince people that the way to move forward is to start developing Targets.

What you will need to be able to do is start to spot what it is that God is doing among the young people in your Targets and to start shouting about it to anyone who'll listen. I always find it helpful to gather as a team after each evening of contact work to discuss what we have seen God do. We get excited about the smallest looking green shoots poking up from the ground that suggest that God is at work in young people's lives. In many places, the very fact that we as a church are actually meeting with non-Christian young people is enough to get people in the church, and to get a youth group, excited.

When we were trying to go from having just a few Targets to moving our entire youth work to operate in this model, we went through a period of ruthlessly sharing only the stories from the Targets, even if sometimes they seemed less exciting. Since testimony acts as prophecy for those who hear it, the very act of sharing what God was doing in the Targets was prophesying other Target visions to be birthed in people's hearts.

You will need to be creative and ruthless in the stories and prophecies you share as you lead up to multiplying other Targets out beyond your initial pilots. Share as much as you can as often as you can. One medium we've found to be really powerful for doing this is the use of videos. We took video at quite a few of our initial Targets (with all the correct permissions of course) and showed it to the other young people, to the leaders, and to the wider church. This enabled people to see with their own eyes that what we were doing wasn't complicated, that it wasn't that flashy or clever, and that it seemed very doable for them.

The final reason for sharing testimonies is that people are suckers for wanting to be a part of where the exciting action is. People are rarely inspired to come and fill a rotation out of a sense of obligation, but they are prepared to give their lives to a cause where they feel like, however hard it is, they are part of fulfilling God's Kingdom plan. With this in mind, don't feel like you have to make it sound like a bed of roses. Be honest and share the struggles, but also share how it feels when you see young people make little stumbling steps toward meeting with their Savior for the first time.

Step 6: Launch multiple Targets

At this point, it's time to bite the bullet and start some more communities with a bigger proportion of your youth and leaders getting involved. You don't have to have every single person on board, but if you've done step five sufficiently, then you'll find that the majority of people are champing at the bit to be a part of what's going on.

The key at this stage will be to get the majority of your youth team to buy into the vision of planting Targets. A good way of doing this is to take the leaders away for a vision and retreat weekend. It may well be worth getting them to read this book before they go on retreat because it will massively help them to catch the vision about what could potentially happen. The leaders retreat itself will give you a chance to effectively recast the vision to the leaders and take them all through a vision-setting process. Hopefully, you will come out of this vision weekend with the vision set for a number of Targets that will largely prioritize making contact with friends of the young people you already have. It will be great for the majority of your leaders to pick a couple of young people with whom they have good relationship and to spend time with them developing the vision and therefore the contact strategy. The visions for these Targets don't need to be fully formed long-term-strategy concepts with three-page vision documents and a website at this point. It might be helpful at the retreat to run through the vision you started the pilot community with, as well as some more stories about what God has already done through it. You may also want to take leaders through the vision flowchart outlined in step three, as this should help them think through what they are doing.[15]

As you share these visions with the young people who are currently not engaged in Targets, but whom you'd like to now get involved, it will be important that you don't just try and socially engineer which communities they join. The temptation at this point is to force the young people to join the Targets that you think they should join. Resist this temptation! Remember that one of the key concepts of Targets is for them to be strongly youth driven. In this early phase of planting Targets, adult leaders usually have to be more strongly involved to get the Targets cranking along. But this creates the danger of losing one of the core concepts before you even get going. If you start a whole bunch of mini youth groups where the leaders decide everything, then you'll simply multiply your workload rather than your youth work.

Step 7: Decide what to stop

Step seven is often the hardest step in the whole process. It's hard because it involves sacrifice, and no one ever likes sacrifice. When we were transitioning the youth work at St. Thomas Philadelphia in Sheffield, we reached a point when we had to bite the bullet and stop what had been the most successful youth event the church had run in the last few years. The majority of our teenagers went to this event and really liked it. The biggest

---

[15] Another great resource that you can get for your leaders is the Leaders Mini Four Cs Guide. We wrote this guide with Target leaders specifically in mind. We give all of our Target leaders a copy of this guide to read, as it helps them to stay on target with their Targets

problem with it was that it served a largely neighborhood vision but wasn't based in that neighborhood. This meant that we had clashes between the needs of the young people who drove to the event from the rich suburban areas and the young people who walked to the church from the local inner-city estate, as I discussed earlier in the book. We knew that the only way to turn the event into a Target was to work alongside the young people to create a vision.

As the leaders of this event talked with the young people from the leafy suburbs, we discovered that the basic gist of the evening worked really well for them. They enjoyed the majority of the activities, and they said that they would have liked to have invited their friends. The leaders then pressed the young people on why so few of them had actually invited their friends. The answer was twofold: First, the kids from the inner-city estate sometimes threatened them. This was something that they said they could cope with but didn't want to risk their friends experiencing; The second issue was that it was difficult to get their friends to the event. Most of their friends lived close to them in the same suburban area, so they needed to drive to get to the event. They told us that it was hard enough to get their friends to come to something at church, let alone getting them to make their parents bring them. One of our amazing leaders (a guy called Phil Joyce) came up with the brilliant plan of stopping the youth event at the church and moving it up the hill into the middle of the area where these young people lived. He worked alongside the young people to come up with a new name and vision and told them he was moving the youth club and also transitioning it to be a Target.

This might sound like it was an easy process, but we actually came under a lot of fire for it. Some of the parents whose young people lived close to the church were angry because their kids had lost their youth club. Some of the Christian parents from the suburbs were angry because they felt that we were taking their young people out of a missional situation and putting them in a less missional place. Other people just seemed to like complaining and hadn't stopped to listen to the vision properly—they had just heard that the club was closing. All of these fears began to be alleviated as we actually started the new Targets and the parents saw how their kids were both happy and living out missional callings to their natural peer groups.

Although stopping is a horrible process, it is also a vital one. You will need to stop something in order to successfully develop your Targets. If you simply try to build Targets on top of the work that you already have, then you'll just burn everyone out. A good way to decide on what central events or activities you are going to stop is to use the M&M lens as a tool.

Use this Table below to help you work it out. List all the programs you run that aren't Targets and that aren't going to be transitioned into Targets in the left column. This may include training, services, events, socials, etc. Then answer the questions in the following columns.

Name of event or activity	Does it help our Target be **missional**?	Does it help our Targets be **multipliable**?	Outcome: Keep or stop. (Justify your answer.)

Once you have decided what you are going to stop, you will need to consider how you are going to communicate this. You will need to consider youth, team members, and parents in your communication strategy. The key with this process is to communicate quickly. Don't tell them six months before something is going to stop that it's going to stop. As soon as you open your mouth to explain what is going to happen, that event is as good as dead in the people's minds. If you give too long of a lead time, you also open the opportunity for people to feel like they have the right to be involved in the process, and they may try to change your mind. Tell them, and actually stop reasonably close to the time you first told them the event was coming to an end.

Step 8: Focus on the center

You should now be ready to start looking at what your central events, training, and systems are and how well they are working. It's tempting at the beginning of this process to start by trying to work out what it looks like at the center, but it's important to make sure that the center serves the Targets. This can't happen if the Targets are designed around what you have at the center.

Once the Targets have begun to work and produce fruit, it is really important to create centralized events, activities, training, and support structures focused on helping these Targets develop because this can be key to multiplication and to enable stability in growth. The key change in mindset when planning out the centralized events is that events and structures at the center must be seen entirely through the M&M lens and through the eyes of how they will support the Targets.

All too often, if the initial steps of this process haven't been taken correctly, then the Targets will gradually support the events rather than the other way around. As a result, the energy will gradually be pulled away from the Target, and you'll end up organizing big events at church and wondering why you're doing it.

We don't do any events or central activities without filtering them through the lens of whether it is going to help the Targets that we have move through the 4 Cs. As a result, the events can come and go, but the principles remain, giving us multipliable DNA throughout the youth work.

Now let's look at some suggested centralized events, support structures, and training, as well as how you may think about using them in your own context.

Start training days

Every six months, we gather Forge leaders from across the network for a training event. These events are necessary to ensure that the missional DNA remains throughout the organization, so leaders attend these training events even though they take our team away from working with young people. We have settled on one packed training day every six months. This is the only training we run that I insist all our leaders attend. The training is less about me transmitting didactic information to our leaders and more about drawing out the vision and strategy for the team.

At these training days, I usually teach the core DNA and values of the 4 Cs. We also use this opportunity to go through some of the key child-protection systems with the teams. All our leaders then do an exercise designed to help them work out where they are in the 4 C process.[16]

Once the youth leaders have worked out the reality of where they currently are, we get them to dream about what their Target would look like if God did immeasurably more than they could ask or imagine and multiplied it. I make them literally write down how many young people they currently have and how many they would have if they multiplied the group by 30, since this is the lowest biblical figure of growth we should expect: *Still other seed fell on good soil, where it produced a crop—a hundred, sixty or thirty times what was sown.* (Matthew 13:8.)

Once they have worked out how many young people they would have after this growth, they then discuss in their teams using this metric: If this were to happen, what should we start, stop, change, and develop?

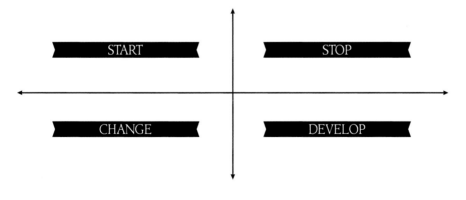

---

[16] This is the same exercise I outlined in step one of this chapter. Our Target leaders do this exercise every six months as part of our training days.

Once leaders have spoken out in faith and have had a strategic session to think about what they would have developed, they can move into making a six-month plan. We deliberately give our youth workers the largest chunk of the day to dedicate to this task. Most youth workers and teams are fantastic at dreaming, having faith, and coming up with creative ideas. But all too often, these get forgotten in the grind of everything else they are doing because they never make a realistic strategic plan that helps them put these ideas into action.

Every six months, then, we get to hold our youth teams accountable to their own plans so that we can help them work toward the Kingdom multiplication growth that God has in store for us.

Create an amazing support structure

One of the hardest structures to get right is your system of support and safeguarding. It is important that we simultaneously provide the highest quality of safeguarding, supporting, and protecting the young people and youth workers we work with while maintaining a relatively light load. This is so that we don't make everything grind to a halt because everyone is spending all their time filling out forms.

Safeguarding and protection procedures will be specific to the place where you work (both your church and your local area). You will need to find out what you need to do to provide the highest quality of care. We have worked very hard on creating a secure online system that youth workers fill out on the fly on a smartphone. This system gives us feedback on every Target that each leader runs. It helps them constantly reflect on what they are doing and also means the central staff gets an email about every event that takes place. This way, we can check that there are no significant problems and that the youth workers are keeping to our systems.

We also get youth workers to fill out a form on our website every time they have a significant conversation with a young person in which they give out advice for their life or where they feel the young person has made a significant disclosure. This protects the youth worker because it creates a record of where they met the young person and what both the young person and the adult said. Having written accounts also means central staff can see if any situations develop in which we need to help a youth worker because the things that a young person has shared may require more specific help than a standard volunteer can provide. You can see all of these forms on our website: www.forgenetwork.co.uk.

A Connection event — Glory Revolution

One of the toughest parts of the 4 Cs process for the Target leaders is the connection part. We have found time and again that the leaders are brilliant at contact and community but struggle when it comes to helping their young people to make the decision necessary for the connection part of the process to effectively work. As stated previously, we have found that a big event is very effective in doing this.

If you have just a few small Targets, then the best thing to do initially is to look around at what events others are already doing. If someone is already doing an event for you, then there is no point reinventing the wheel.

If you are larger and can manage your own events, then the process is actually very simple. First, work out what will draw a crowd among your young people. Music is the obvious way to go, but it's not the only way. Second, preach the gospel with all your might. Third, do an amazing job of response. I have been to so many Christian events where someone presents a fantastic message but then leaves everyone unsure of what they are supposed to do about it. Make the response the most obvious thing in the world.

I usually say something like, "If you believe what I said is true, and you want to meet Jesus for the first time, then come to this place right here right now." Then take a deep breath and wait and trust that they will come. It's a bit of a leap of faith, but after you've seen it work many times, you start to trust that the Good News really is good news!

The last thing about running these connection events is that you need to brief all the leaders clearly before the event. Make sure they know that if any of their young people respond, they should come with them, lead them to Jesus (you may want to help them with what to do), and then meet up with them no longer than 48 hours later to start to process what God has done. The moment they give their lives to Jesus, the enemy will try and snatch that seed of faith before it gets anywhere near growing into full-blown, life-changing faith, so immediate processing is key.

A Commission event — Redefine

Once you have a few Christians across all your Targets, it is wise to begin to think about how you can support multiplication through a commission event. This event needs to be held in an inspiring training environment that helps the top young people grow in leadership and faith so that they are ready to lead the next wave of Targets as you multiply.

These events should not run too frequently. We run ours three times a year, and this is the most often I would consider doing them. The schedule needs to allow the young people space between events to try out everything they have learned.

Also, these events don't need to be complicated in terms of the program at all. I suggest gathering for worship, teaching, action, and discussion. We always have a time to worship God together at the beginning to ensure that we are not simply pushing our young people into trying to do it all on their own but instead framing the day by worshipping our awesome God. The teaching is usually extremely challenging and focused on how we are stepping out in the things that God has for us.

We always send the youth out to do something that really challenges and pushes them. This doesn't have to be something that they will want to continue forever, but it should help them learn and grow. The event then finishes with a time to process everything they have learned and a conversation about how they are going to use the leadership skills they have gained and put them into practice in their Target and in their context.

Step 9: Create team structures and financial models

While this next step doesn't sound very exciting, it's a really important part of the process. At this point, you will have Targets that are beginning to spread across your town, city, or rural area. Your central team structures will be developing to support all that is going on. At this point, it's time to start thinking seriously about how you have structured your team and how you are going to financially support the growth that you will see when multiplication occurs.

Team structure

You need a team structure that can support a growing network of Targets. The overall leader of the youth work can become a significant bottleneck at this juncture unless you create a good team structure and support model. I learned about this bottleneck the hard way as our Targets began to multiply and the number of leaders became increasingly hard for me to personally invest in and support. We needed a team structure that would support growth into the future, so I implemented a broken-down structure that looked like this:

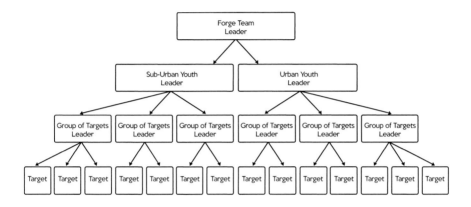

This structure was multipliable because it was easy for my two top leaders and their teams to implement it as they connected, trained, and communicated across all the Targets for which they were responsible. You can't necessarily copy the way in which I chose to break our teams down, but you will need to work out how you are going to structure your team so that, as you grow into the future, your top tier of leadership remains small enough for you to invest in.

Huddles

We have found that the best way to invest in our teams is through the huddle structure. Huddles, which are discussed in Mike Breen's book *Building a Discipling Culture*, are the best vehicle we have found to develop our leaders once we have created a good structure. The huddle system works as the main leader invests in a small number of key leaders, and then this cascades down the chain as those key leaders invest in their leaders, and so on. This Huddle system is something we have to constantly work on, and we use the systems and methods that Mike describes in his book. I recommend getting this book and implementing a huddle structure among your leaders.

Finances

Youth work is expensive; it is sadly and simply part of life. Our youth work runs at a fraction of the cost of most secular youth work projects, and yet it still costs nearly 100,000 pounds a year[17] when you include all the salaries and operational costs of the Targets and the big events. Our church is not able to sustain a youth work budget of this size, so we have to constantly learn how to drive an economic engine that allows the youth work to grow and develop.

At this point in your journey, you are going to need to pay serious attention to how you are going to keep growing without being curtailed by running out of money. We have learned many ways to do this, but the most valuable piece of advice I can give is to try not to become too dependent on one resource method. Even if the church or organization that you work for has lots of money to invest in youth work, you never know when that situation might change. We learned this the hard way when one of our major backers suddenly cut our funds, leaving us several thousands of pounds short of what we needed to pay everyone's salaries for the year. This experience was actually good for us because it made us develop a wider portfolio of financial sources, including our local government, the local police authority, personal gifts from individuals, Christian trusts, the local church at St Thomas Philadelphia and secular funding pots. We try and raise smallish amounts of money from all of these sources in order to keep growing the ministry of Forge into the future.

You don't need to copy our method, but you will need to do research into your locality to discover where your funding might come from. Remember not to be afraid to ask non-Christians for money toward youth work. Even they love to see young people's lives turned around, so of course they want to invest in you!

---

[17] That's more than $150,000 for you Americans.

Step 10: Crank the multiplication using M&M

By this point, you will be seeing young people coming to faith through your Targets, new Targets starting to form and grow, and events and team structures supporting growth. That means you're ready to crank the handle of multiplication. This is an exciting time, but you as a leader need to keep three key rules in mind in order to ensure that the multiplication process works well:

1. Tell people to multiply before they actually have to

The most painful part of the process for everyone is when multiplication occurs. As mentioned previosuly, we have a rule in Forge that when your Target gets to 30 people, you have to start considering how you are going to multiply. Lots of leaders really struggle with this, but you need to hold to this as a key part of the DNA of what you are building. If you allow your Targets to become too fat, they cease to be able to multiply at all, and you'll need a huge earthquake to fix it. You have to remember that you are actually helping leaders by making them multiply sooner rather than later.

To help do this, make sure that you are working hard at commissioning the young people properly. The biggest mistakes we have made with Targets happened when we have left them for too long or let them get too big without forcing the issue of multiplication with our leaders. Multiplication doesn't just happen by chance; you need to call for it from the top, and you need to support, equip, and challenge leaders to make sure they follow through.

2. Don't drop the ball on multiplying leaders

Your youth work can only grow at the pace at which you call, multiply, and develop leaders among both adults and young people. If you want to keep cranking the handle of multiplication, then you need to consistently keep processing how well you are creating leaders. Keep looking for ways of calling more adults into the team. Train all your leaders (both adults and young people) to be excellent at calling people to come and be a part of what God is doing in their Target.

One of your key resources is leaders, so investing a significant amount of time in them is well worth it. As multiplication starts to happen and the busy time kicks in, it will be tempting to not bother with Huddles, leader weekends, and team retreats. But these things are vital in maintaining a good rolling movement of youth work.

3. Keep the culture through language

We have found the Lifeshapes language, coupled with a continual focus on the 4 Cs and the M&M lens, are the best ways to keep hold of a culture as everything multiplies. We remind our leaders of these key foundations every six months at our leader training days. We also give every new leader a Target leaders guide to the 4 Cs. You will find it helpful to have this resource in bulk so that you can give it out regularly to your team to keep everyone on the same page and pushing forward with the same culture despite vast differences in the work that every Target is doing.

Through all the steps

One final thing to mention is that it's important to measure the right things as you consider how successful you are. You are looking to make disciples, not fill up youth events. Often, youth workers measure all the wrong things to try to determine how effective they are. We need to measure numbers of communities, numbers of disciples, and how effective we are being at creating this journey.

When we measure how well we are doing across Forge, we add up the number of young people on the fringe of all of our Targets (currently for us, it is nearly 800), the number of young people committed to a discipleship Target (currently a little more than 600), and the number of Targets we are running for these young people (currently just under 30). You should also be able to say which of the 4 Cs is the major priority across the whole spectrum of the youth work. For us, the priority is currently commission, but this is constantly changing.

It's been a brilliant ride for us here in Sheffield, and I believe the 10 steps we took on this ride will help you take it too. As one final resource, here is the timeline of when each of these steps should happen in progression in order to reach multiplication within a two-year timeframe.

TARGET TRANSITION TIMELINE

Time to start the step at:	Steps:
START	Step one
One month	Step two
Six weeks	Step three
Two months	Step four
Eight months	Step Five
Nine months	Step six
One year	Step seven
14 months	Step eight
20 months	Step nine
Two years	Step ten

CHAPTER 8

CONCLUSION

I'm convinced that running Targets, missional communities, or whatever else you want to call them is the most effective way of reaching young people and creating disciples. I'm convinced that you'll have amazing fun as you lead a bunch of young people on a journey that you'll never forget; they won't forget it either.

I was writing emails the other day when I got a Facebook message from one of the young people who was in one of my early Targets. She wasn't in the Target for more than a year, and she had never come to faith before she moved away. Well, she is all grown up now (man, it made me feel old), and she wanted to tell me that she had joined her local church because all she had learned with us had somehow clicked. Her first child had even just been baptized. It's so amazing to hear the stories, even of the young people who seemingly got away. God still manages to take hold of their lives if we invest in making contact with them, building community, connecting them to Jesus, and commissioning them to go and live the life. The very simple message of this guide is that you need to keep movement in the youth work that you are running. Following these stages seems to me to be the best way of staying on target.

As I sum up the end of this book, I look back on five massively exciting years. True, there were highs and lows, fun times and hard times, but overall it has been such a privilege to be part of everything that God has been doing here. Despite all that we've seen God do in the last few years, I know that there is so much more for us to do.

The latest statistic tells us that 73 percent of young people who attend college as Christians quit their faith within nine days. Nine days! This inspires me all the more to share the importance of running youth work that not only reaches the lost but that also disciples young people to live out the great new life that Jesus has won for them. My hope is to see a generation of Christian young people going to university and expecting to transform the place with the love of Jesus rather than giving up because they can't find a church with the right music within nine days.

It's time for our young people to forge a different path. Let's lead them to be able to pursue their academic careers having seen their whole friendship group come to Jesus so that they already know what they need to do when they get to campus. They don't even need to find a church because they know that they can always start one!

Resources

We've created a whole load of resources that will help you as you lead. These include:

- ✖ Truth Revolution (a six-week introduction to Christianity DVD for new Christians)
- ✖ Leaders 4 Cs guide (a short guide with the 4 C principles for Target leaders)
- ✖ Lifeshapes for Teenagers (coming soon)

You can find out how to get these resources on our website at www.forge. co.uk.

Go for it

All we can say in conclusion is GO FOR IT! Set up your Target and have an amazing adventure with a bunch of young people.